Critical Acclaim from Successful Business Warriors

Who's the enemy? That's the first question any marketing strategy should deal with. Don Hendon's new book demonstrates how marketers need to use military thinking to achieve marketing objectives. Well-written and right on target.
— AL RIES, author of *Marketing Warfare, Positioning,* and *War in the Boardroom*

Donald Hendon proves he's a warrior with the quality of his information and proves he's a winner with the quality of his writing.
— JAY CONRAD LEVINSON, bestselling author of *Guerrilla Marketing*

Don't just survive in the 21st century — discover how to thrive and explode your business. This book will give you the tools, strategies, and weapons you need to out-think and out-maneuver your competition.
— KURT MORTENSEN, author of *Maximum Influence* and *Persuasion IQ*

Business is a battle. It's a battle for ideas, for strategies, for differentiation, for efficient communication, and for implementation. It's a battle for margins, for ROI, for the hearts and minds of the customer. Don Hendon's *The Way of the Warrior in Business* is the blueprint that will enable any business to win. If you follow Don's advice, I guarantee you it will really be Mission Accomplished.
— BOB PRITCHARD, BSc, CSP, AISMM. International Marketer of the Year

Donald Hendon's new book, *The Way of the Warrior in Business,* is a great read that should be studied by every business person and business student.
— ROGER DAWSON, author of *Secrets of Power Negotiating*

A very fresh work on marketing. It's transformational — it will change how you lead your company. It goes far beyond any other book that's out there now in its practical and useful construct. Very well worth reading, not only for you but for everybody on your sales and marketing team.
— MITCHELL GOOZÉ, author of *The Secret to Selling More* and *Value Acceleration*

If you want to win, I mean *seriously* beat your competition, read this book! *The Way of the Warrior in Business* shows you how to think, act, focus, and conquer like the best military leaders, except from the comfort of your home. If I had three thumbs, they would all be up!
— SCOTT DEMING, branding and marketing expert, international speaker, trainer, and best-selling author of *The Brand Who Cried Wolf*

Using Don Hendon's techniques, I made HK $1.5 million extra the very same week!
— P. J. FANNING, Director, Jardines Engineering Corporation, Hong Kong

If you are looking for a tool chest of proven ideas to generate and keep more business, this book will get you there faster than any resources I know.
— ARNOLD SANOW, MBA, CSP, author of *Present with Power, Punch, and Pizzazz!*

I just can't praise Don Hendon's book enough for bringing a fresh insight to the challenging world of marketing. *The Way of the Warrior in Business* is a very impressive book! Very highly recommended!
— MICHAEL AUN, author of *It's the Customer, Stupid!*

Don Hendon does an excellent job of updating the earlier work of Ravi Singh, Al Ries, Jack Trout, and myself on how the metaphor and strategies of warfare can be applied brilliantly to win competitive business battles.
— PHILIP KOTLER, S. C. Johnson and Son Distinguished Professor of International Marketing, Kellogg School of Management, Northwestern University

My experience as a U.S. Marine has been of incalculable help in my business career. Even if you're not a leatherneck, reading this marvelous book will endow you with the warrior's edge that you need to be successful. Don't wait to be drafted ... buy it now!
— ED BRODOW, author of *Negotiation Boot Camp*

Warrior-like businesses have a huge advantage today, because they are nimble, quick, and always on the offense. If your business is stuck in a rut, this book will get you into the warrior mindset. Your competition will fear you!
— TIM VAN MILLIGAN, CustomerSecrets.com

After reading Don Hendon's *365 Powerful Ways to Influence,* I had to get *The Way of the Warrior in Business.* This guide is a no-holds-barred battle plan for winning the war in business. And if that sounds too aggressive to you, be warned that anyone of your competitors armed with Hendon's weapons is already planning on how to take your business off the playing field. With examples from Sam Walton (whom the author knew) of Wal-Mart fame and Mao Tse-Tung's battle strategy that won him rule of China, one can't help but come away with larger dreams than before starting this book.
— JAMES DILLEHAY, co-author of *Guerrilla Multilevel Marketing*

Buy Don's book and learn his tried-and-true ways to win once a day for a year, and you will be a better influencer for it.
— MARK J. RYAN, Mind Body Expert, MarkJRyan.com

Did you ever think that "being a warrior" meant "being macho?" Wrong! Did you ever think that a stronger brand always beat a weaker brand? Wrong! Did you ever imagine that becoming more like a child could help you become a winner in business? Right! These are just three of dozens of powerful "warrior" insights that Don Hendon gives you in his powerful new book.
— STEVE SAVAGE, co-author of *Guerrilla Business Secrets* and author of *Savage Sales Secrets*

Not since the book *Art of War* has a book so unapologetically provided a path to victory!
— DAVID FAGAN, Icon Business Development and Cutting Edge Ventures

Don Hendon's *The Way of the Warrior in Business* is absolutely unique, dense with vital information, and battle-tested in the real world of executives and corporate wins and losses. What else would we expect from an expert who has taught tens of thousands of executives in 36 nations on 6 continents? Read the chapter titles alone and you won't be able to resist buying the book. His thinking about Mao and Sam Walton will more than give you your money's worth. As a psychotherapist, I know that lack of assertiveness is the under-estimated enemy of the psyche. This book is a literal arsenal of assertiveness.
— BOB BEVERLEY, EmotionalElegance.com

Marketing is war!!! *The Way of the Warrior in Business* is your guide to strategic and tactical planning and execution that gets you ahead of your competition. The same strategies that win wars are applied to the war of business and marketing. Start winning by reading this essential resource.

— KRISTA NEHER, bestselling author of *The Social Media Field Guide* and *Visual Social Media Marketing*, international speaker, trainer and educator

It's easy to get stuck in a rut when looking for new marketing ideas. Don's unique approach to marketing will help trigger new ideas, insights, and possibilities for competitive advantage. *The Way of the Warrior in Business* will make you jump up and do something!

— JIM THOMAS, professional negotiator and bestselling author of *Negotiate to Win*

The war in healthcare is about shifting from a mindset of illness to one of wellness. It's a good war to fight, one battle (patient) at a time. That is why Dr. Hendon's *The Way of the Warrior in Business* should be a top read for healthcare CEOs and board members.

— ANTHONY CIRILLO, FACHE, ABC

There are a lot of books on the market claiming to offer the latest sage advice on marketing, but only a few that can actually help you to become a better marketing professional. *The Way of the Warrior in Business* is that book. Don's book is packed with solid marketing strategies and real-world examples and techniques to close more deals. Hendon captures a lifetime of successful marketing strategies and experiences and presents it in a practical approach for anyone who is involved in marketing. In today's hyper-competitive economy, where the primary focus is on winning new business, this is a must read.

— DOUG DVORAK, Founder & Managing Principal, DMG International

The Way of the Warrior in Business can be of use to all those looking to change their marketing mindset and grow their pipeline of customers.

— RICHARD WEYLMAN, Managing Director and Board Chairman, Weylman Consulting Group

The author cleverly shares a variety of business principles and tactics by helping business owners think and act like a member of the military. The warrior likes to win and be on top in every situation, just like those fighting for business in a crowded, competitive market. If you want to be a winner, then *The Way of the Warrior in Business* should be an essential addition to your business library. The book is way more than filling your quiver with arrows. It's insightful, thought-provoking, and sure to help you re-think the way you gain and maintain your competitive edge.

— MARTHA GUIDRY, Principal, The Rite Concept, and author of *Marketing Concepts That Win!*

Marketing Warrior Don Hendon has created a captivating battle plan for winning the business marketing war. Make no mistake, if you are in business, you are at war — not just with competitors, but with apathy, anonymity, commodity, and visibility. Read this cleverly crafted book to learn how to develop your strategy to not just survive, but to win the battle for business.

— DAVID AVRIN, author of *It's Not Who You Know, It's Who Knows YOU!*

Don's *Way of the Warrior in Business* will give you a needed crash course in the strategy and most importantly the gritty *how-to* tactics to improve your business now! Get your highlighter out and get ready to enjoy this amazing book.
— CHIP EICHELBERGER, Top 5 motivational speaker, GetSwitchedOn.com

Unconventional. Consistent. Effective. Don Hendon explains the rules of marketing through the eyes of a military leader, then trains you on mastering them as tactics, weapons, and winning strategies. On their path to becoming Business Warriors, all marketers should assimilate and use this knowledge. Perfectly adapted for the new economy, valid in any territory, Europe included.
— ALEXANDRU ISRAIL, Guerrilla Marketing Master Trainer, MarketMinds, Romania

A powerful book that will change your business forever. Highly recommended.
— DR. FERMIN J. CASTILLO, JR., Professor of Marketing and HRM, University of Jazeera, Dubai, United Arab Emirates

In 400 BC, Sun Tzu wrote about how to defeat the enemy in his book *The Art of War.* His writings turned out to be invaluable lessons for savvy marketers around the world on how to gain market share from their competition. Well, after 2500 years, it's time to take these principles and make them more relevant than ever for today's marketplace. In *The Way of the Warrior in Business,* Don Hendon defines what it takes for battle-scarred marketers to lead their motivated organizations by understanding the enemy (competition). He clearly lays out how to get your marketer to do what it takes to stay well out in front in order to strengthen your market share and brand strategy. This book should be one of the tools taken into every business planning meeting of an aggressive, successful company.
— KEN BANKS, CEO, KAB Marketing, Retail Advertising Hall of Fame

Don has been there, seen it, done it, and figured out how. He gives clearly thought-out strategies and techniques you can immediately use to obliterate the competition.
— ALAM GHAFOOR, author of *Innocent Terrorist* and one of U.K.'s master negotiators, influencers, and deal-makers

Everything you need to know to be a big winner in contemporary strategic marketing is in this book.
— JACK LIM, Publisher, *World Executive's Digest,* Manila, Philippines

The title says it all: *The Way of the Warrior in Business.* Don Hendon takes you through basic training, strategy, tactics, and surprise. He even throws in 365 winning weapons. Get this book and go on the offensive.
— DAN POYNTER, author of *The Self-Publishing Manual*

Comprehensive and insightful, *The Way of the Warrior in Business* will carry you to the winner's circle through learning and applying its effective strategy and tactics. Don Hendon has nailed it when it comes to understanding what it takes to win in business! I thought I was good when it comes to business, but I've learned more through this book than any I've read in years. This is clearly a must read!
— CHUCK GALLAGHER, author of *Second Chances: Transforming Adversity into Opportunity* and *The Human Factor: A Common-Sense Approach to Creating a Culture of Ethics in the Workplace*

If you aren't selling *every day,* you're losing ground to your competition and losing the opportunity to innovate. Seasoned marketers and novices will find in *The Way of the Warrior in Business* many fascinating insights that successful companies use to win. I think you'll find it an extraordinarily valuable reference book.

— FRANK MCKINNEY, bestselling author of *Make It Big* and *The Maverick Approach to Real Estate Success*

Jump-start your thinking. Read Don Hendon's *Way of the Warrior in Business* — and do it before your competitors do. Take it to heart. Implement his insights and create the results you want.

— RICK FRISHMAN, founder of Planned TV Arts

Modern business meets the ancient art of war! Donald Hendon's *The Way of the Warrior in Business* is a brilliant read that takes you from Sun Tzu to Mao Tse-Tung all the way up to Sam Walton of Wal-Mart fame. From attacking the flank to outmaneuvering your opponent, Hendon shows how generals develop strategy and how soldiers carry out tactics. A must-read for all business leaders who are fighting for market share in today's hyper-competitive economy.

— JEFF BEALS, award-winning author of *Self Marketing Power* and *Selling Saturdays*

Don Hendon's *Way of the Warrior* is filled with practical wisdom and straightforward tools that work! Get it, read it, and win big!

— FORD SAEKS, CEO, Prime Concepts Group, Inc.

Don Hendon's approach to marketing is refreshingly thorough. Marketing is a skill that can be learned when you have the right mindset. Using Don's strategies to develop a mindset that supports business growth, you will be able to effectively attract more clients, make more money, and gain more leverage in your industry. Well done.

— DARNYELLE A. JERVEY, MBA, CEO of Incredible One Enterprises LLC

Insightful, strategic, and profitable. These are but a few words that describe Don Hendon's new book, *The Way of the Warrior in Business*. Contained in this powerful book are blueprints on how you can grow your business, win more customers, and dominate your marketplace. If you can read only one book from cover to cover this year, read *The Way of the Warrior in Business*. It will transform you into a true warrior in your business.

— JOHNNY CAMPBELL, DTM, aka The Transition Man

Why would I endorse a fellow competitor's book? The answer is simple: It's that good. Many people are shocked by warrior reference in a business book, but often business is a war—why do you think they call it a price war? *The Way of the Warrior in Business* provides a realistic approach to meet today's business challenges. Following Hendon's advice will guide you through the challenges you face. While no book has all the answers, Hendon's book points you in the right direction, making it a must-read.

— TED GARRISON, New Construction Strategies, industry expert, and construction business visionary

Looking for a way to fight and conquer your next marketing objective? Look no further — *Way of the Warrior* has all of your answers. This book should definitely be used to help develop your next master plan.

— MIKE MINTER, CEO, Minter Enterprises

After reading Don Hendon's latest book I have found a true resource for every sales leader and salesperson. Each chapter is jammed with ideas and tools that can be easily implemented to improve the professionalism of your team. With my clients I recommend that at least twice a year the entire sales team read a sales book and weekly discuss each chapter — their own book club! I am adding Don's book to my list — you should too.
— KEN THORESON, SalesManagementGuru.com, AcumenManagement.com

This book is an absolutely essential reference tool for anyone who is serious about the sales profession. It should be read and referred to on a regular basis.
— JOSEPH SHERREN, CSP, HoF, author, speaker, trainer

Don Hendon once again has brought forward a must-read, step-by-step guide on how business owners can win in the game of business. As he likens the precision of military campaigns to the battlefield of capitalism, Hendon teaches his readers that it takes strategy, tactics, philosophy, and a clear goal in order to reach objectives.
— AARON S. YOUNG, CEO, Laughlin Associates, author, speaker, teacher

Growing a company and making a profit today is tough. In *The Way of the Warrior in Business,* Don Hendon shows you how to out-flank your competitors and become the best in your market place. I highly recommend this book to anyone who wants to learn the steps to win the war for more profitable revenue.
— GEORGE HEDLEY, Entrepreneur of the Year Award Winner and owner of Hardhat BIZCOACH.

Don lays out a most unusual approach to achieving success in business. Read it before your competitors do, and make a big difference in your future. It will be your go-to guide for years to come!
— DR. JOHN GIBSON, author, *Family Matters Matter*

Using analogies from classic successes in military and business warfare, in his *Way of the Warrior in Business,* Don not only shows how to develop a winning strategy, he delivers high-impact and solid real-world examples, along with tactics, techniques, and tools any business can use.
— ALLAN KARL, WorldRider, adventurer, keynote speaker, author, and entrepreneur, AllanKarl.com

Satisfy your inner general and open up this book.
— TRON JORDHEIM, CMO StorageMart

The single biggest mistake businesses and executives can make is to assume that the market — where competitors fight for customers — is a level playing field. Don Hendon's book is a valuable reminder to both small and big companies and the executives who work for them that the only way to win customers is by constantly training to be a warrior.
— GAURAV BHALLA, Ph.D., author of *Collaboration and Co-Creation: New Platforms for Marketing and Innovation*

THE WAY OF THE WARRIOR OF THE WARRIOR IN BUSINESS

THE WAY OF THE WARRIOR IN BUSINESS

Battling for Profits,
Power, and Domination
— And Winning Big!

Donald Wayne Hendon

FOREWORD BY PHILIP KOTLER

MAVEN HOUSE
PRESS

Published by Maven House Press, 316 W. Barnard St., West Chester, PA 19382; 610.883.7988; www.mavenhousepress.com.

Special discounts on bulk quantities of Maven House Press books are available to corporations, professional associations, and other organizations. For details contact the publisher.

While this publication is designed to provide accurate and authoritative information in regard to the subject matter covered, it is sold with the understanding that the publisher is not engaged in rendering legal, accounting, or other professional service. If legal advice or other expert assistance is required, the services of a competent professional person should be sought. — From the Declaration of Principles jointly adopted by a Committee of the American Bar Association and a Committee of Publishers and Associations

Library of Congress Control Number: 2013934518

Paperback ISBN: 978-1-938548-06-2
ePUB ISBN: 978-1-938548-07-9
ePDF ISBN: 978-1-938548-08-6

Printed in the United States of America.

10 9 8 7 6 5 4 3 2 1

CONTENTS

1   Basic Training

When business executives know and use military strategies and tactics, their market share, sales, and profits greatly increase. Learn how to develop the killer instinct that turns innocent lambs into powerful business warriors who win big and win often. Jump-start your mindset here, and you'll start thinking and acting like a well-oiled military machine.

2   Strategy, Tactics, and Surprise

Target competitors who are easily conquered. Win by distracting, deceiving, and confusing them. Learn how to make them make mistakes. Surprise them — play upon their fears, make them feel trapped.

3   Planning, War Games, and Winning Big

Become the 800-pound gorilla in your industry by smart planning. Learn your risk profile — are you a falcon, sitting duck, chicken, or dodo bird? Find out about the "So what?" analysis — the most insightful analysis you'll ever make. See the best war games on the market today.

4   Winning the Battle for Your Customer's Mind:
The Three Ps of Marketing

Discover the Three Powers of Marketing Warfare. Learn how well-fortified weaker brands can do a lot more than repel attacks from Big Dogs — how they can actually defeat them. Don't be macho — learn why attacking the leader head-on usually leads to disaster, why it's so important to be first in the market, and what you can do if you're not first.

5   Out-Thinking Your Competitors:
The Creative Business Warrior

Learn the 20 characteristics of creative people and the six characteristics of the creative company. If you're not that creative, this chapter gives you many ways to become a lot more creative.

LIST OF FIGURES

FOREWORD

Philip Kotler

The S.C. Johnson & Son Distinguished Professor of International Marketing, Kellogg Graduate School of Management, Northwestern University

In the late 1960s, marketing executive J. Hugh Davidson built successful brands at several U.K. companies, including Procter and Gamble, Playtex, and United Biscuits. In 1972, he told the world how he did it in the very first marketing warfare book ever written, *Offensive Marketing*, published by Cassell. His ideas in a nutshell: Make the first move — go on the offensive by continually innovating. Don't react defensively to competitors' moves — anticipate them, and counter-attack immediately. Don't imitate them. Within a few years, an American consulting company, Advanced Management Research, began using his ideas in a series of seminars under two titles: *Marketing Warfare* and *Attacking the Competition*.

The term *Marketing Warfare* soon caught on. Ravi Singh (Achrol) and I wrote an article with this title in the Winter 1981 issue of *Journal of Business Strategy*. We discussed and evaluated five attack strategies: frontal attack, flanking attack, encirclement attack, bypass attack, and guerrilla attack. We also evaluated five defensive strategies: position defense, mobile defense, pre-emptive defense, flank positioning defense, and counter-offensive defense.

We pointed out that business people in that era frequently used military talk to describe their situations: "There are price wars, border clashes, and skirmishes among the major computer manufacturers; an escalating arms race among cigarette manufacturers, market invasion and guerrilla warfare in the coffee market. A company's advertising is its propaganda arm, its sales reps are its shock troops, and its marketing research is intelligence. There is talk about confrontation, brinksmanship, super-weapons, reprisals, cut-throat competition, and psychological warfare. Companies talk about going to battle, invading markets, and returning fire with fire."

We also pointed out that warfare analogies and principles apply in many critical decision areas, including determining objectives, developing attack strategies, and developing defense strategies.

In 1984, Jay Conrad Levinson borrowed ideas from Mao Tse-Tung and he wrote *Guerrilla Marketing*. This book and over 50 spin-offs have sold 20 million copies over the years. In 1986, Al Ries and Jack Trout published their *Marketing Warfare*. In 1987 Donald Wayne Hendon weighed in with *Battling for Profits*. Over the years, other books appeared from such authors as Gerald Michaelson (Sun Tzu — *The Art of War for Managers*, 2001), William Cohen (*Art of the Leader*, 1990), and Dan Kennedy (*No B.S. Direct Marketing*, 2006).

Truly, things are a lot more competitive now than they were 40 years ago. Today, many executives may *think* they're being aggressive, but too often, they're still simply reacting to competitors' moves. We think that Donald Wayne Hendon, in *The Way of the Warrior in Business*, will help change their mind-set. This book will help them deepen their understanding of military strategy doctrines and also remember that a military consciousness must not replace the more basic marketing consciousness. Reading it, mastering its principles, and implementing its strategies and tactics will help them win most of their battles.

INTRODUCTION

This book is about marketing. It's about knowing and using military strategies and tactics to increase your profits, your power, your ability to dominate your market. Read it, master its principles, take it to heart, and by implementing its strategies and tactics you'll not only become a Business Warrior — you'll become a victorious Business Warrior!

As you go through the 11 chapters, you'll learn many things, such as:

- How to apply the ideas of such military geniuses as China's Sun Tzu, Japan's Miyamoto Musashi, Vietnam's Le Duan, China's Mao Tse-Tung, Britain's Basil H. Liddell Hart, and Germany's Karl von Clausewitz to your own business

- Never interrupt your competitors when they're making a mistake

- Win your business war not by dying for your country — win it by making the other poor bastard die for his country

- Your risk profile — are you a falcon, sitting duck, chicken, or dodo bird?

- How to become more creative — become more like a child

- Why Sam Walton is the ultimate guerrilla

- Where to look for and find competitors who are easy to conquer — they're really easy to find

- 365 very powerful and unique tactics — including how well-fortified weaker brands can not only repel attacks from big-name brands but actually defeat them

- How to get big by thinking small

- How to win in each of the four battlegrounds of business

Finally, this book isn't just for sales and marketing executives. Military officers and enlisted personnel who are ready to retire can use this book. It tells them how they can use what they learned in their military careers to succeed in their next career — the business world. Very ambitious military people at the beginning of their careers will also find this book valuable. They will find business strategies and tactics in this book that will help them get promoted often and faster.

So, business warriors, get out your highlighters and start on your journey of discovery — or re-discovery — of marketing warfare.

Don Hendon
GuerrillaDon.com

Basic Training

Business is not just *similar* to war — it *is* war! Executives are always trying to improve their position in the market place. They share this belief: My market share will have to come at another company's expense. It's a zero-sum game. A rising tide still lifts all boats, but the tide is no longer rising. Instead, businesses are fighting one another for the right to stay in the lifeboat. More fighting means business has become more warlike. And business executives can learn much from the military. That's what this book is all about.

Knowing and using military strategies and tactics will increase your market share, sales, and profits. What you're about to read is based on a seminar I've given to thousands of people throughout the world, *Business Warfare,* and now it's in book form — you're holding it in your hands right now. Let's start calling it *your* book. Your book will help you become a big winner in business.

How wars are fought has changed dramatically over the centuries. They last a much shorter period of time — unless you're fighting guerrillas. They will wear you out. You'll get a big kick out of Chapter 8, "Winning Business Warfare the Guerrilla Way." (By the way, my nickname is Guerrilla Don. Learn more about me by going to my website, GuerrillaDon.com.) At the same time, today's modern business can no longer take decades to build. Time and timing are critical success factors.

Similarities and Differences between Military and Business Battles

In business and military situations you'll find:

- There are two or more sides.
- Each side struggles to increase its power.
- The power increase is at the expense of the other side, the enemy.
- Enemies use all kinds of weapons to injure their opponents.
- They maneuver for advantage by preparing carefully designed campaigns that include firepower (low pricing, creative distribution, personal sales blitzes, product development, new packaging, etc.), dirty tricks, decoys, traps, and an entire arsenal of weapons. Furthermore:

The Military Wants To:	Business Executives Want To:
Destroy a target	Eliminate a competitor
Defend a position	Defend market share
Seize the high ground	Invade an attractive market
Win the hearts and minds of the people	Increase brand awareness and loyalty and improve product approval ratings

In your business, do you talk like military people do? If you use many of these phrases, you're in a real war, and this book will help you increase your market share and profits:

- Invade new markets
- Border clashes
- Skirmishes
- Sabotage
- General staff meetings
- Intelligence
- Hate the enemy
- Price wars
- Guerrilla warfare
- Spying
- Outflank
- Propaganda arm

- Confrontation
- Superweapons
- Psychological warfare
- Brinksmanship
- Reprisals

Now, don't take this too far. There are big differences between the military and business:

- *Differences in constraints.* Military battles are fought with very few limitations on weapons. Government and public opinion have placed many restraints on businesses, including laws concerning price discrimination, misleading advertising, etc.

- *Differences in objectives.* Military battles are fought to achieve total victory — to destroy the enemy completely. Most businesses don't want to destroy a competitor, especially because of anti-trust laws.

Look at this continuum:

| Collusion | Outward Cooperation | Peaceful Coexistence | Cold War | Hot War |

The military and businesses are very much alike at the right-hand side and least alike at the left-hand side.

Collusion happens when two or more firms have secretly agreed to not compete in certain areas — geography, price, product introductions, etc. This is illegal in many nations. However, many nations allow cartels to divide the market. Cartels are groups of independent businesses that have formally joined together to limit competition or fix prices. Each member of the cartel then has a monopoly in its area. Is your firm here? If so, you probably don't need to read this book — unless you think things will change soon.

Outward cooperation takes place when different companies in an industry act in concert in their advertising, product development, pricing, sales promotion, etc. Usually, the industry leader acts first, and the rest follow shortly afterwards. This is common under conditions of oligopoly — where there are a few large sellers and many buyers that are much smaller than the sellers. All companies feel the interest of all is best served by acting together.

Peaceful coexistence, sometimes called *fair competition,* occurs if no firm is out to destroy or really damage another. This occurs in many industries. What about your industry?

A *cold war* happens when major companies engage in frequent skirmishes. To improve their market shares, firms are ready, willing, and able to hurt their rivals. They think of them as enemies. The harm stops after a certain point, though, because most businesses are somewhat scrupulous. This kind of business warfare occurs in mature industries, such as the soap/detergent, consumer appliance, and rubber tire industries. Here, total industry sales are falling, and a firm can gain only at the expense of others. Is this what happens at your company?

A *hot war* doesn't happen very often in business — at least it hasn't in the past. Hot wars may become more common in the future if firms become bent on dominating through continuous battles. Dominating means different things to different firms — from destroying all the competition to forcing all competitors into major concessions and compromises. In a hot war, you become unscrupulous and you're prepared to use dirty tricks and cover them up so that the government and other authorities won't discover what you're doing. Chapter 11 lists 81 dirty tricks used in negotiating. They can be applied to business warfare, too.

How Badly Do You Want to Win?

Do you have the *killer instinct?* I divide killer instincts into five categories: Machiavellian, Company Politician, Survivalist, Straight Arrow, and Innocent Lamb. If you're in the first two categories, you probably want to win very badly already, and you're best equipped, mentally speaking, to fight and win a business war. If you're a Straight Arrow or Innocent Lamb, you'll probably lose most business wars you fight.

And fight you must. This may be the exact opposite of how you were raised and what you were taught in grade school. In grade school, there are no bad guys, everyone is special, and bullying is inappropriate behavior. But in the world of business, *there are bad guys, the most special guy wins, and bullying happens.* If you can't accept these facts, maybe you shouldn't enlist in the Business Army.

In the 1800s, the German philosopher Heinrich von Treitscheke said, "Your neighbor is always ready to better himself at your expense." Michael Korda says in his book *Power!,* "Your interests are nobody else's concern. Your gain is always somebody else's loss. Your failure is someone else's victory." All life, in fact, is a game of power. The world is a challenge and a game, and a sense of our own power is at the heart of it. The object of the game is to find out what you want and then get it. The moves of the game are complicated, and they make up the core of Business Warfare. Read the rest of this book and prepare yourself for the fight to come! And it will come! Hey, watch out, maybe it's here already!

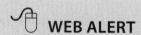

WEB ALERT

Go to GuerrillaDon.com where you can take a test to see whether you have the killer instinct or not.

You should want to win the fight, because winning is powerful. And being powerful is the ultimate goal of the fighters of this world. Powerful people will keep their jobs and will get promoted. Their company will benefit, will make money, and stay in business. If you don't fight, you may not get promotions or pay raises because the company's sales aren't growing. You may even get fired.

Some people play the power game for money. Some for security or fame. Others for sex. Most for some combination of these objectives. But the master players seek power itself, because they know that power can be used to obtain money, security, fame, or sex. So if you want a lot of those four things, you must win — you must try to be Number One in your industry.

Lessons from Winning Athletes

Athletes have the winning instinct, and many of them turn into good executives because of this instinct. They know there can be only one Number One, and that nobody remembers who Number Two was. All of us remember the first girl or boy we kissed, but how many of us remember the second? All of us remember who won last year's Super Bowl. But how many of us remember who lost?

If you're a football fan, you've heard about Vince Lombardi, who reached the zenith of his power with the Green Bay Packers in the 1950s and 1960s. Some criticized him for his "win at any cost" attitude. I never did. I love his philosophy of winning. Lombardi said:

> Winning is not a sometime thing; it's an all-the-time thing. You don't win once in a while, you don't do things right once in a while, you do them right all the time. Winning is a habit. Unfortunately, so is losing.

There is no room for second place. There is only one place in my game, and that is first place. I have finished second twice in my life at Green Bay, and I don't ever want to finish second again. There is a second-place bowl game, but it is a game for losers played by losers. It is and always has been an American zeal to be first in anything we do, and to win, and to win, and to win.

Every time a football player goes out to ply his trade, he's got to play from the ground up — from the soles of his feet right up to his head. Every inch of him has to play. Some guys play with their heads. That's OK. You've got to be smart to be Number One in any business. But more important, you've got to play with your heart — with every fiber of your body. If you're lucky enough to find a guy with a lot of head and a lot of heart, he's never going to come off the field second.

Running a football team is no different from running any other kind of organization — an army, a political party, a business. The principles are the same. The object is to win — to beat the other guy. Maybe that sounds hard or cruel. I don't think it is.

It's a reality of life that men are competitive, and the most competitive games draw the most competitive men. That's why they're there — to compete. They know the rules and the objectives when they get in the game. The objective is to win — fairly, squarely, decently, by the rules — but to win.

And, in truth, I've never known a man worth his salt who in the long run, deep down in his heart, didn't appreciate the grind, the discipline. There is something in good men that really yearns for and needs discipline and the harsh reality of head-to-head combat.

I don't say these things because I believe in the *brute* nature of man or that men must be brutalized to be combative. I believe in God, and I believe in human decency. But I firmly believe that any man's finest hour — his greatest fulfillment to all he holds dear — is that moment when he has worked his heart out in a good cause and lies exhausted on the field of battle — victorious.

You've got to pay the price to be Number One. Are you on the team? The *winning* team?

Lombardi's philosophy was a winner's philosophy. You could do a lot worse than to adopt his words as your own philosophy of life. Be a winner! It's a lot more fun than being a loser!

The Importance of Marketing

If you're skimming this book at the bookstore to see if you want to buy it or not, you've probably noticed something. You're reading about marketing, not about the other two major functions of business. There are only three things a business does:

- It makes something. That's the production function. Engineers predominate here.

- It pays for what it makes. That's the finance function. Finance people and accountants predominate here.

- It passes along what it makes to somebody else — wholesalers, retailers, and final consumers — at a profit. That's the marketing function.

So if you're involved in marketing, this book is for you. But even if you're in production or finance, you'll learn a lot from this book. Because the techniques you'll read here are much broader than marketing. Anytime you try to get people to do what you want them to do, you'll use these techniques. You can call them business warfare techniques. You can call them persuasion techniques. You can call them influence techniques. You can call them manipulation techniques. Check out Chapter 11, pages 181–210. It's a list of business warfare techniques you can use in many areas:

- Getting your kids to pick up their clothes
- Flirting and seducing
- Changing your vacation date at the last minute
- Getting a raise or a promotion
- Buying a house
- Selling a car
- Dealing with a hostile attorney
- Getting out of a traffic ticket
- Sellers — getting buyers to pay more
- Buyers — getting sellers to lower their prices
- Getting your staff to work harder and increase their productivity
- Out-psyching bullies

Anyway, throughout this book I'll talk about marketing. Whenever I do, please apply what I say to your own situation. Even to get your spouse to let you play golf more often.

Now, let's talk about the military.

Learning from the U.S. Army

Figure 1.1 shows you what the U.S. Army thinks are the keys to success in fighting wars. These keys to success can be applied to business as well. The objective is to win, and you see this in the inner circle. In the middle circle are things that are controllable: the commander, the troops, their morale, and the resources at the commander's disposal. In the outer circle, the external environment, are the constraints over which the company has no control: terrain, weather, and luck. These uncontrollable elements have a direct bearing on the outcome of the battle.

The commander has three characteristics:

- Personality
- Knowledge — of both his or her troops and the enemy's troops
- Capacity for planning sound strategy and tactics according to the principles of war

If you're the commander, what's your personality like? In particular, how much do you want to win? In business terms, how marketing-oriented are you?

Evaluating Yourself:
How Marketing-Oriented Are You?

There are three kinds of executives:

- Production executives — they make things.
- Finance executives — they are in charge of paying for things the company makes.
- Marketing executives — they pass products on to customers at a profit.

The Business Warriors who read this book are marketing-oriented. They're the ones who want to win! Production and finance people are interested in production efficiency and in the bottom line. They aren't too interested in how the product gets to customers.

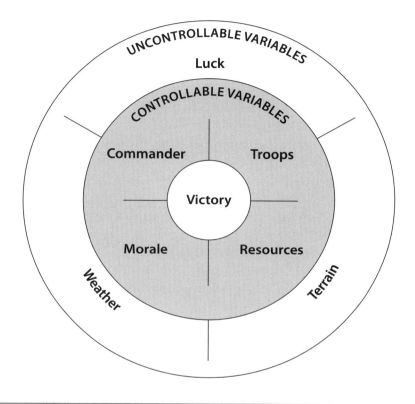

Figure 1.1. The U.S. Army says "This is what it takes to win"

Are *you* production-oriented, finance-oriented, or marketing-oriented? Let's find out.

Answer the twenty questions below. Don't think about the answers too much. Instead, answer them right off the top of your head. Be as honest as possible with yourself. Remember, nobody will see your answers but you. Answer these questions the way you would behave if you were managing a group of people at the office. Put one of these letters in each of the blanks:

A = All the time
O = Often
S = Sometimes
R = Rarely
N = Not at all

Say to yourself, "If I were the manager of a company team, I would:"

_____ 1. Take a hand in monitoring each member's career

_____ 2. Minimize suggestions from employees on how to improve their job design

_____ 3. Offer rewards and additional incentives for good work done

_____ 4. Listen to employees' complaints about inequities in the pay scale

_____ 5. Be reluctant to correct subordinates in an objective and direct way

_____ 6. Create opportunities through which employees could realize their potential

_____ 7. Make my presence felt on the job and make sure things are done right

_____ 8. Hold private face-to-face dialogs with employees to find out how they feel about their jobs and the company

_____ 9. Make sure employees know and understand what is expected of them

_____ 10. Keep the size of teams small enough so that supervisors and members will get to know each other well

_____ 11. Delegate additional responsibilities to employees who welcome additional work

_____ 12. Ensure that performance targets are reasonable and realistic

_____ 13. Be inaccessible for questions, suggestions, or complaints

_____ 14. Rush in and take over when the job gets out of hand

_____ 15. Push for support from higher management in putting our team's plans and projects into action

_____ 16. Find out what employees value the most and reward them on the basis of that information

_____ 17. Share power and responsibilities with the informal leaders of the organization

_____ 18. Consult only my co-managers in solving production-related problems

_____ 19. Make my team members contribute in setting up performance standards for both quality and quantity

_____ 20. Get ideas on improving job procedures from first-line workers

Here's how to determine your score. Give yourself one point only if you answered this way. Zero points if you answered any other way:

_____ 1. A or O		_____ 11. A or O
_____ 2. R or N		_____ 12. A or O
_____ 3. A or O		_____ 13. R or N
_____ 4. A or O		_____ 14. R or N
_____ 5. R or N		_____ 15. A or O
_____ 6. A or O		_____ 16. A or O
_____ 7. A or O		_____ 17. A or O
_____ 8. A or O		_____ 18. R or N
_____ 9. A or O		_____ 19. A or O
_____ 10. A or O		_____ 20. A or O

Next, add up your scores this way: Put the scores you entered above in the appropriate blanks below, add up your scores (for customer concern and sales concern), and put that sum in the Total blanks.

Score for Customer Concern	Score for Sales Concern
_____ 1.	_____ 2.
_____ 4.	_____ 3.
_____ 5.	_____ 7.
_____ 6.	_____ 9.
_____ 8.	_____ 12.
_____ 10.	_____ 14.
_____ 11.	_____ 15.
_____ 13.	_____ 18.
_____ 16.	_____ 19.
_____ 17.	_____ 20.
_____ **TOTAL**	_____ **TOTAL**

Figure 1.2. The marketing-orientation matrix

Now, look at Figure 1.2. Locate yourself on the marketing-orientation matrix. Take your total score for customer concern from above and find it on the concern-for-the-customer axis at the bottom of the matrix; draw a vertical line through your score and up the matrix. Then take your total score for sales concern from above and find it on the concern-for-making-the-sale axis at the left side of the matrix; draw a horizontal line through your score and across the matrix. Put an X where your two scores intersect. You'll be in one of five categories:

- Take it or leave it (worst)
- Marketing-oriented (best)

- Formula seller (not bad — middle of the road)
- Hard seller (extremely vicious, prone to using dirty tricks). You'll read 81 of these in Chapter 11, pages 204 – 210.

- Appeaser (extremely passive, prone to using submission tactics). You'll read 16 of these in Chapter 11, pages 201 – 202.

If you're not now marketing-oriented, I'll show you how to become more marketing-oriented in this book. If you're already somewhat marketing-oriented, I'll show you how to improve.

The Marketing-Oriented Business Warrior

I hope that you found out that you are marketing-oriented. Let's see what this means.

If you or your company are marketing-oriented, you have adopted the marketing concept. Some of you old-timers may remember Burger King's old slogan, "Have it your way." It's a simple concept, yet many executives and companies have never put it into practice. It says you have to start with the customer. Determine his or her wants and needs. Then, decide which wants and needs, if any, you should try to satisfy *at a profit*. Next, do everything you can to profitably satisfy them through a company-wide marketing effort. Keep profit in mind, not just sales volume, as your final objective.

Your *entire* company should be dedicated to satisfying the customer at a profit — that should be its reason for existence. That's easier said than done, though. In companies that aren't marketing-oriented, each department runs its own affairs for its own benefit. In meetings, each department head has one overriding idea (objective): protecting the department's interests. These companies are full of empire-builders, who see other departments as revolving around them. Sometimes they even think of other departments as enemies who are trying to get more share of a limited budget — at their expense! This attitude creates conflict. And the marketing department is often involved in these conflicts because other departments often have strong opinions about marketing decisions. Figure 1.3 points out some of the differences between marketing departments and other departments.

Marketing Department	Factors to Be Considered	Other Departments
Features that sell	Product features	Engineering: Functional
Nonstandard	Parts	Purchasing: Standard
Tight	Quality control	Production: Average
Intuitive	Rationale for spending	Finance: Strict
Special terms, discounts	Transactions	Accounting: Standard
Minimum credit examination	Customer's financial disclosure	Credit: Full disclosure
High stock level	Inventory	Storage: Economical stock level

Figure 1.3. How marketing departments see things differently from other departments

The Hard-Seller

Some of you may think this is a good category to be in. It isn't. High pressure tactics alienate customers. However, if your business doesn't depend on repeat customers, this is a good position to be in. But most of you depend on repeat sales. You don't come to town one day and leave the next, taking the money and running. If you are overly concerned with getting orders, you are not marketing-oriented because you may be giving away profits for volume, thinking that volume alone will make you look good. Figure 1.4 points out some of the fundamental differences between marketing and selling.

The Appeaser

If you're in this category, you need to become more sales-oriented. You are *much too* customer oriented. You like people so much that in order to get them to smile at you, you'll give away the store! That's as bad as the hard seller who wants volume instead of profits. You need to become more sales-oriented. As the Beatle's song said, "Money can't buy me love."

Marketing	Factors to Be Considered	Selling
On wants, needs of customer	Emphasis	On product or service
External — toward market's needs	Orientation	Internal — toward company's need to sell more and more
Customer wants and needs; then figure out how to make and deliver product to them at a profit	What comes first — product or customer wants and needs	Product; then figure out how to sell it at a profit

Figure 1.4. Fundamental differences between marketing and selling

The Take It or Leave It Person

This is the worst possible category to be in. If you're here, you probably don't give a damn about anything. You're like an amoeba, just existing, waiting around listlessly. You probably will never be a success, unless you change dramatically. Obviously, you have much to do. Start with your attitude. It desperately needs changing.

The Formula Seller

People in this category are already oriented toward making the sale and satisfying the customer, but they haven't gone far enough. They are still inexperienced. Their goal is to be marketing-oriented, so they have to develop their tendencies toward that prime position on the matrix.

Beginning sales reps are usually taught formula selling, especially in some industries. Take insurance, for instance. Some companies tell the new sales rep to memorize a canned sales pitch and repeat it word-for-word in every situation, because 40 percent of the time, it will result in a sale. The new sales rep tries it, and it works about 40 percent of the time, so the rep is happy. The only trouble is that it's not flexible enough. If a prospect interrupts the canned pitch, sometimes the sales rep won't remember where he or she left off and will have to start all over again. Moving to the marketing-oriented category is easiest for formula sellers, because they're already inclined in the right direction.

Moving Forward: Your Plan of Action

If you're marketing-oriented, move on *now* to the other chapters to learn how to maximize your profits and potential.

If you're a hard-seller, an appeaser, somebody who says "Take it or leave it," or so inexperienced that you rely on formula selling as a crutch, you need to become more marketing-oriented to be a winning Business Warrior. How can you become more marketing-oriented? These six steps can help you. Put them into a plan of action — and implement it!

1. Re-read this chapter so you'll know what marketing-oriented really means.

2. Keep an open mind. Be open to new possibilities and to the fact that you don't really know everything there is to know and that you can learn from others.

3. Devise a plan to achieve your goal. You know yourself. You have to develop your own plan because you know your own strengths and limitations. Tailor your plan, building upon your strengths, acknowledging your limitations, and trying to overcome them.

4. Build in motivation. Try to visualize the benefits you'll get from being a winner in business, be it money, security, fame, or something else. Get excited about the possibility of being a winner! And get others excited about it, too. Your spouse, girlfriend, or boyfriend can be a big help here because they can inspire and motivate you when you are down on yourself. Bosses can help motivate and inspire you as well when they realize your improvement will make them look even better.

5. Give yourself periodic evaluations. Check your progress toward your goal.

6. Modify your goal if necessary. Perhaps you'll have to be satisfied with only a partial movement toward being marketing-oriented the way the big winners are.

Eventually you'll become so marketing-oriented that you'll do the right thing unconsciously. It may take a while, though, for you to become unconsciously skillful at being a winning business warrior. Figure 1.5 shows you the learning path you'll need to take.

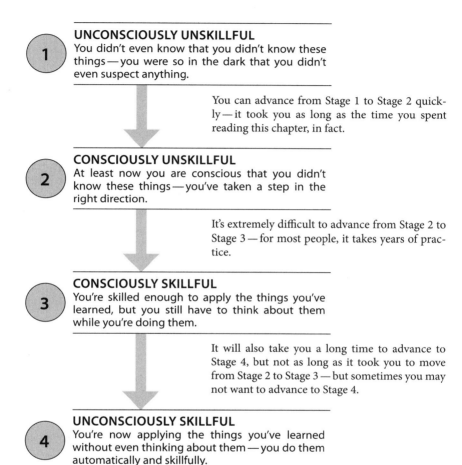

1 UNCONSCIOUSLY UNSKILLFUL
You didn't even know that you didn't know these things—you were so in the dark that you didn't even suspect anything.

You can advance from Stage 1 to Stage 2 quickly—it took you as long as the time you spent reading this chapter, in fact.

2 CONSCIOUSLY UNSKILLFUL
At least now you are conscious that you didn't know these things—you've taken a step in the right direction.

It's extremely difficult to advance from Stage 2 to Stage 3—for most people, it takes years of practice.

3 CONSCIOUSLY SKILLFUL
You're skilled enough to apply the things you've learned, but you still have to think about them while you're doing them.

It will also take you a long time to advance to Stage 4, but not as long as it took you to move from Stage 2 to Stage 3—but sometimes you may not want to advance to Stage 4.

4 UNCONSCIOUSLY SKILLFUL
You're now applying the things you've learned without even thinking about them—you do them automatically and skillfully.

EXAMPLE: If an American moves to Australia for a two-year period and knows for sure that he'll return to the United States in exactly two years, he may not want to become unconsciously skillful at driving on the left side of the road as the Aussies do. Why? Because it will be that much harder to adjust to driving on the right side of the road again when he returns home. So, he may just want to stay at the consciously skillful stage while in Australia. While I was a visiting professor there for two years, I stayed at Stage 3 by continually talking to myself while driving, "I have to stay on the left, but this is not real." For most important things, you should want to reach Stage 4 eventually—most winners have reached this stage in the business world.

Figure 1.5. You learn in four stages

2

Strategy, Tactics, and Surprise

S trategy is deciding *what* to do. Tactics is deciding *how* to do it. In other words, strategy is doing the right thing. Tactics is doing things right. Managers at the very top should pick the strategy to use. Managers at lower levels should decide on the tactics to use to implement the strategy their bosses picked. Yes, it's that simple. Or is it?

But before you begin reading this chapter, look briefly at Chapter 6. It's the one most concerned with strategy. And look briefly at Chapter 7. It's the one most concerned with tactics.

Sun Tzu's Ideas

Sun Tzu (pronounced Soon Zzuh), a great military general in China, wrote *The Art of War* around 500 BC. It has influenced military thinking to the present day. Mao Tse-Tung often bragged that he memorized Sun Tzu's book. You will read many quotations from Sun Tzu throughout this book because the principles he established long ago still apply to winning business wars today. Here's how Sun Tzu differentiated between strategy and tactics.

Strategy

You may think you're the best if you win all the battles you fight, but you're wrong. The best thing to do is to mess up your enemy's strategic plans. The second best thing is to keep your enemy's spread-out forces and allies from concentrating in one point against you. The third best thing is to attack your enemy's army in the field. The worst thing to do is to lay siege to walled cities (in marketing terms, going after a strongly entrenched competitor with a big market share). Attack a walled city only if there's no alternative.

The most skilled warriors defeat enemy troops without *any* fighting at all. They capture walled cities without assaulting them. They conquer enemy kingdoms without long, drawn-out operations in the field. The most skilled warriors completely triumph over the enemy without losing one single soldier. With forces completely intact, they become masters of their enemy's empire. This is what strategy is all about.

Tactics

All warfare is based on deceiving the enemy. Make them think you're unable to attack, when you're really able. Make them think you're inactive when you're really using your forces. And if *they* are inactive, give them no peace. Make them think you're far away when you're really near, and vice versa. Use baits to lure them into traps. If they think you're disorganized, you can crush them. If they're well-fortified, prepare for them. If they're stronger than you are, evade them. If they have a bad temper, provoke them into rash moves. Make them cocky and arrogant by pretending to be weak. If their forces are concentrated, separate them. Become like ghosts in the moonlight by appearing where you're not expected and by attacking them where they aren't prepared for you.

Don't Confuse Strategy and Tactics

Sometimes it's hard to see the forest because the trees are in the way. Too often top managers who should concentrate on strategy concentrate on tactics instead. Why? Because the problems with the shortest time horizons, the tactical problems, tend to win the battle for the top managers' time and attention. There are four reasons for this:

- Tactical problems are routine and repetitive.
- Tactical problems are brought to management's attention by lower-level managers and by management reporting systems as a matter of routine.
- Tactical problems happen often and in large volumes.

- Tactical problems are familiar and even comforting for managers to deal with because they have had previous training and experience at lower levels of the organization where operating decisions are the sole concern.

Who's Responsible for What?

Here's a rule of thumb: Those who are higher in the business organization decide on strategy, while those who are at lower levels decide on the tactics to be used to implement the strategies. It's relatively easy to sit back, think, and pontificate on the overall strategy to use, but it's difficult to choose and actually perform the tactical maneuvers. It's that way in the military, too. The great 19th century Prussian general Carl von Clausewitz said warriors "require more special knowledge in tactics than in strategy." He also said, "The means and forms which strategy uses are in fact so extremely simple, so well known."

Here's what I say: Those who have risen high in the organization have moved up because they were good at performing the difficult, dirty work — the tactical maneuvers. They were so good at it, they got promoted, and then they used their knowledge of tactics as an aid in choosing the right strategies. Just as you can't be a good sales manager without first being a good sales rep, you can't be a good strategist without first being a good tactician.

Although strategy is easier to master than tactics, the risk of being wrong is greater at the strategic level than at the tactical level. And that's why managers at the top (strategy) get paid a lot more than lower-level managers (tactics). The risks they take are greater. If they're wrong, the company loses much more than if the wrong tactical maneuver is executed. So if you're at the bottom of the totem pole, take heart. If you survive your difficult years, you'll find it easier when you are paid big bucks to decide on strategies. If you want to get to the top faster, though, you need to begin to study strategy now. This will prepare you for the next big step in your career. The rest of this chapter concentrates on strategies rather than on tactics.

Surprise and Distraction

I call it surprise. Sometimes I call it distraction. Liddell Hart calls it the indirect approach. Sun Tzu calls it deception. Read on and decide what you want to call it.

Liddell Hart's Distraction Strategy:
The Superiority of the Indirect Approach

Who is Liddell Hart? He was a distinguished British soldier who has influenced military thinking probably more than any other person in recent years. Full name: Basil H. Liddell Hart. Born 1895, died 1970. His extensive writing on military strategy and tactics is required reading at West Point, Sandhurst, and other leading military schools throughout the world. Because his thoughts are so important to winning business/marketing wars, he deserves a special section in this chapter on strategy.

Liddell Hart said this: The indirect approach is superior to the direct approach. What is the indirect approach? It's the "unsuspected infiltration of a different idea or by an argument that turns the flank of instinctive opposition." Why? Because "the direct assault of new ideas provokes a stubborn resistance, thus intensifying the difficulty of producing a change of outlook." In other words, surprise or distract the enemy and you'll win!

Sun Tzu, as usual, comes to the point more quickly. He said, "It's easy to pick a fight. Use the direct approach. But if you want to win, you must use indirect methods."

Liddell Hart stresses over and over again the superiority of the indirect approach. He said it's a philosophical truth that can be applied to any problem "where the human factor predominates, and a conflict of wills tends to spring from an underlying concern for interests. In commerce, the suggestion that there is a bargain to be secured is far more potent than any direct appeal to buy. As in war, the aim is to weaken resistance before attempting to overcome it. And the effect is best attained by drawing the other party out of his defenses."

Why is this true? Look at it this way: When you approach your opponent directly, along the line they naturally expect, you are only consolidating their balance. This increases your enemy's power of resistance. Liddell Hart used an analogy from wrestling here: The attempt to throw the opponent without loosening their foothold and upsetting their balance results in self-exhaustion. Success by such a method only becomes possible through an immense margin of superior strength and, even so, tends to lose decisiveness. In most campaigns, the dislocation of the enemy's psychological and physical balance has been the vital prelude to a successful attempt at their overthrow.

How do you lower your enemy's resistance? Dislocate them. I call this "distract them." How? Check out the 22 Distraction Weapons under Assertive Weapons in Chapter 11, pages 186 – 187. They're pretty simple to follow — and very effective.

What Several Military Warriors Say About Distraction

Sun Tzu didn't call it distraction—he called it deception. He said that those called skillful in war conquer an enemy who is easily conquered. Because they deceived the enemy. So we should confuse our enemy. Their confusion is a product of our perfect discipline. So we need a good organization. Their cowardice is a product of our courage. So our troops need to be full of latent energy. Their weakness is a product of our strength. So our tactics must work. When all this happens, our enemy will be deceived and move the way we want them to move.

U.S. Army general George Patton said that the way to win a battle is not to die for your country. The way to win a battle is to make the other poor bastard die for *his* country.

Liddell Hart said don't go out looking for trouble. Instead, reduce the enemy's possibility of resistance. When this happens, you'll win without any serious fighting. How so? When you "dislocate" him, either he will become dissolved or he will be easily disrupted. His forces will become too widely distributed and too committed elsewhere, so he won't have the freedom to counterattack.

Civil War general T. J. "Stonewall" Jackson put it in simpler terms. His motto was "Mystify, mislead, and surprise."

How Do You Dislocate and Distract Your Enemy?

By movement and surprise. Movement is physical movement. Surprise is not physical—it's the psychological manipulation of your enemy's will. Movement generates surprise, and surprise gives impetus to movement.

Movement. Make your plans based on three things: Time, the marketing environment, and the movement and maintenance of your marketing forces. Here's what movement does for you:

- It upsets your enemy's concentration of marketing forces because you have suddenly changed the front.
- It separates your enemy's marketing forces.
- It endangers your enemy's supplies.
- It menaces your enemy's escape routes.

Surprise. Psychologically surprising your enemy is a lot harder than physically moving your marketing forces. This is how you do it:

The best way is to make your enemy feel trapped. If they realize your movements have suddenly placed them at a disadvantage, and if they feel unable to counter your moves, you have strategically dislocated them by surprise.

Remember that suddenness is extremely important in marketing and military wars. Delaying even an instant may mean the difference between winning and losing. Sun Tzu had much to say about this:

- Make sure you win a quick victory. If it takes too long to decisively defeat your enemy, your weapons will grow dull, and your troops' morale will go down.

- When you besiege a walled city, it takes such a long time to wear down the enemy that your troops' strength is eventually exhausted.

- When all this happens, when your weapons are dull, when your troops' morale is low, when their strength is exhausted, and when all your treasure is gone, other close-by enemies (competitors) will take advantage of your poor position and attack you when you are at your weakest. Then, nobody, even if he or she is the wisest person in the world, will be able to avoid disaster.

- Although we've heard of stupid haste in battles, it's equally stupid to have long delays before decisively winning.

- Speed is the essence of battle. Be sure you take advantage of your enemy's un-readiness, travel using unexpected routes, and attack them where they have taken no precautions.

Liddell Hart said that one of the easiest ways to distract your enemy is to play upon their fears.

The Pros and Cons of Attacking Your Enemy's Rear

In war, the enemy's rear is their weakest point. In marketing, this means striking at your competitor's weakest market position. Think about it this way: People can't defend their backs from a blow without turning around to use their arms in the new direction. The same thing with an army. *Turning* temporarily unbalances an army. And an army remains unbalanced for a much longer time than a person does.

On the other hand, if you move directly against your enemy, what happens? Your enemy consolidates their physical and psychological balance, and this increases their power of resistance. In other words, the longest way round (attacking the rear, which is attacking your competitor's weakest market position) is often the shortest way home (to victory). Why? Because physically, you have found the *line of least resistance*. And psychologically, you have found the *line of least expectation*.

But things are not that simple. Let's say you're attacking your competitor's weakest market position: their rear. Unless you do it quickly and surprise your enemy, you're not using an indirect approach anymore. You may start out indirectly, because you're not attacking your enemy's strongest point (the front). But the very directness of your progress toward their rear weak point will alert your enemy to your intentions. This allows your enemy to physically augment their marketing forces. And so what started out as an indirect approach soon becomes just another direct approach to a new front, because you lost the element of surprise.

Don't Make Dumb Mistakes

Dislocation must precede your attack. You can't hit the enemy and be successful unless you've first dislocated them using your two new friends, physical movement and psychological surprise. Exploitation must follow your attack. Your success won't be decisive unless you exploit your *second opportunity*, which comes before the enemy can recover. If you don't follow both of these fundamentals of warfare you'll be making a serious mistake.

Liddell Hart said that these two fundamentals have often been ignored by the military because they stressed tactics instead of strategy. And that's why many 20th century battles have been indecisive. He said, "The training of armies is primarily devoted to developing efficiency in the detailed execution of the attack. Concentrating on tactics obscures the psychological element. It fosters a cult of soundness, rather than of surprise. It breeds commanders who are so intent not to do anything wrong, according to the book, that they forget the necessity of making their enemy do something wrong. Result: Their plans have no result. Why not? Because in war it is by making your enemy make mistakes that the scales are most often turned."

Sun Tzu put it this way: The best warrior wins battles without making any mistakes. You are certain to win if you avoid mistakes, because you're conquering an enemy who is already defeated. If your army makes any of the mistakes below, it's your general's faults, and these mistakes will lead to your defeat.

- *Flight.* If your general makes you attack a force ten times your size, you'll have to flee.

- *Insubordination.* If your foot soldiers are too strong and your officers are too weak, insubordination will occur. This weakens you and will lead to your defeat.

- *Collapse.* On the other hand, if your officers are too strong and your foot soldiers are too weak, your army will collapse.

- *Ruin.* If your top officers are too independent and hot-headed for their own good, they might get so angry, they'll decide to attack your enemy on their own without waiting for their commander to study the matter and coordinate things. If this happens, the result is your ruin.

- *Disorganization.* If your general is weak, he or she is without real authority. Three signs of this are unclear and indistinct orders, no fixed assignments for the officers and foot soldiers, and sloppy battle formations. When these things occur, the result is complete disorganization. And this weakens you and will probably lead to your defeat.

- *Rout.* If your general doesn't estimate the enemy's strength correctly, uses a smaller, weaker force to attack a larger, stronger one, or doesn't put the best soldiers in the front ranks, the result will be a rout. (Marketing translation: Put your best sales rep in the best territory.)

Napoleon put it this way: Never interrupt your enemy when it's making a mistake.

The Strategic Importance of the Size of Your Market Share

A very large percentage of marketing warriors are convinced that market share is the single most important determinant of profitability. Profits are how you keep score, just as the military keeps score by the number of battles won. Don't be misled by high sales volume. It's ridiculously easy to increase your sales volume — just give your product or service away. But that will decrease your profits. So what's left? Market share, that's what. You've got to dominate your market if you're going to become a really big Business Warrior.

Cultural Mistakes by Business Warriors

When a Business Warrior decides to invade another nation, marketing mistakes are often made because cultures are so different. Here are examples of cultural mistakes:

- U.S. product marketed in Southeast Asia: Pepsodent's slogan, "You'll wonder where the yellow went," was interpreted as a racial slur.

- U.S. product marketed in Indonesia: Gulf No-Nox gasoline (petrol) sounded like the Bahasa word *nonok*, which is Indonesian slang for *vagina*.

- Japanese product marketed in the United States: The Sumimoto Steel Corporation ran ads in several American trade journals, stressing "Sumimoto High Toughness." It used very large letters, SHT, in the ads. Many people inferred SHT to mean *shit*. This was an image Sumimoto did not want to present to Americans.

- British product marketed in Hong Kong: It was difficult for Guinness Stout to reposition itself as a male drink because Chinese women would drink it during their monthly periods to gain strength. To compound the problem, an ad once showed a St. Patrick's Day party in a Hong Kong pub, with people throwing green hats around. At the end of the ad a hat landed on a man's head by accident, and he smiled at the camera. Wearing a green hat in Hong Kong means your wife is cheating on you.

- U.S. product marketed in Mexico: American Motors' Matador automobile was criticized because *matador* means *killer* in Spanish. Social critics said they had enough killers on Mexican roads without adding another.

- U.S. products marketed in Brazil: Ford's Pinto automobile did not go over well at first because *pinto* is Brazilian slang for *a small penis*. Ford changed the car's name quickly. And an American airline was promoting its sophisticated

Rendezvous Lounges on its Boeing 747 jets traveling to Brazil without realizing that *rendezvous* is Brazilian slang for *a room rented out for prostitution.*

- U.S. products marketed throughout South America: Parker Pens used the slogan "Avoid embarrassment, use Parker Pens," without knowing that the word they used for *embarrassment* was South American slang for *pregnant.* A toothpaste manufacturer's slogan, "Be more interesting, use our product," was interpreted as "Be more pregnant, use our product."

- British product marketed in Saudi Arabia: A computer manufacturer was talking about a *dummy load,* which is a computer term, in its ads. In Arabic, the words *dummy* and *load* combined mean *false pregnancy.*

- U.S. product marketed in Canada: Hunt-Wesson decided to expand its line of "Big John" food products to Canada. In Quebec, which is French-speaking, Big John translated to *Gros Jos,* which is French Canadian slang for *big breasts.*

- British product marketed in Italy: Schweppes promoted its tonic water by calling it *oil water,* without realizing that *oil water* is Italian slang for *toilet.*

- U.S. product marketed in Germany: Pepsi used the wrong translation, it seems, in its "Come alive with Pepsi" slogan. Germans interpreted it as "Come out of the grave with Pepsi."

- British product marketed in Germany: Rolls Royce promoted its expensive Silver Mist automobile there, not knowing that *mist* means *shit* in German.

My forthcoming book, *Dumb, Dumber, Dumberest — The Stupidest Business Mistakes of All Times,* gives you 100 categories of dumb mistakes such as these. It shows you two things: How to get out of the trouble you put yourself into by making dumb mistakes and how to avoid making dumb mistakes in the first place. Watch for it! Coming soon.

One executive said this: It is one of our objectives to be first or second in each market. If we can't be number one or two, we will take a good long-term look to see whether we ought to stay in the business. You've got to have some impact in the marketplace or you're always dancing to someone else's tune. They're making the dough, and you're always playing catch-up.

Academic research done over several decades by the Harvard Business School and the Marketing Science Institute agree — the higher the market share, the higher the profitability. Here's why.

The market leader can achieve lower unit production costs and can spread marketing costs over a larger sales volume. As a result, the firm can do a better production and marketing job and still have a better profit left after overhead costs are paid. Number two companies can do well if they have decent market shares. Number three companies can survive, but they won't be too profitable. The remaining firms won't have the sales volume to compete effectively, so they'll continue making inadequate profits and fall further and further behind until they drop out completely.

Many marketers think this way, so the marketing environment has become more and more competitive, much like a military battlefield. Becoming anything less than number one or number two seems to be almost unthinkable in an era of heavier competition.

But you've got to be careful when you define your market share. What share are you talking about? Let's say you're a regional marketer, strong only in the southeastern part of the United States. There you have a 40 percent market share and are a dominant factor. But if you define your market as the entire United States, you may have only a 3 percent market share. It's unrealistic to think you're an underdog with only a 3 percent share, because you're not marketing in most of the United States. A small national share here is misleading. You really have a high enough regional share to make your firm a dominant factor in the marketplace that's relevant to you. And, as you'll learn in Chapters 8 and 9, strategies and tactics for underdogs are much different from those used by Big Dogs.

Moving Forward: Your Plan of Action

First, always remember the difference between strategy (what to do) and tactics (how to do it) and who's responsible for each — top managers are strategists and middle-level and lower-level managers are tacticians.

Second, remember this — you're a Business Warrior who is reading a book about business warfare. So try out some of the military principles that will help you succeed. In addition, read about the best of Liddell Hart and the U.S. Army below.

Figure 2.1 shows a table I present to executives — it's a non-military way to look at differences between strategy and tactics.

Liddell Hart's Eight Principles of Warfare

- Adjust your end to your means. Don't be greedy and bite off more than you can chew. Be confident and optimistic, but not overconfident and overoptimistic. Get a sense of what is possible and probable so you'll be able to face facts realistically. Don't exhaust your confidence in a vain effort that will fail because your eyes were bigger than your stomach. Maintain your confidence for future battles.

- Keep your objective always in mind while you adapt your plan to your circumstances. Make sure you pick the right path.

- Choose the line of least expectation. How? Be empathetic. Put yourself in your enemy's shoes, and try to figure out which course of action your enemy will be least likely to foresee or forestall.

- Exploit the line of least resistance. In strategy, this means you should exploit any tactical success. In tactics, this means you should make the most effective use of your reserve forces.

- Take a line of operation that offers alternative objectives. If you have only one objective, it will be easier for your enemy to figure out what that objective is. On the other hand, if you appear to have several objectives that you're pursuing, you're distracting your enemy physically and psychologically. This gives you a pretty good chance of gaining at least one objective: the one your enemy is guarding the least. As Sun Tzu said, "Never let anybody know where you intend to fight. In that way, the enemy must prepare to fight in many different places, and you will only have to be prepared to fight in one certain place."

WEB ALERT

Liddell Hart's eight principles of warfare are taken from his classic book, *The Strategy of Indirect Approach*, which is available free online. Go to http://bit.ly/hartstrategy.

Strategy	Component	Tactics
Try to force things to happen	Attitude (overall)	Find things to exploit
Long-term success, short-term loss	Attitude (to success and loss)	Long-term success, short-term success
The way the company is organized to produce maximum tactical pressure on competitors	Definition	The way that produces results
Strategy drives the tactics	Dictation vs. Drive	Tactics dictate the strategy
Many	Elements (the number of)	Only one
Unfolds, changes over time	Evolution	Constant, independent of time
Internal	External or Internal (to product/service/company)	External
Build tactics into a strategy	Order	Tactics come first
Product/service/company-oriented	Orientation (#1)	Communication-oriented
Existing markets	Orientation (#2)	New opportunities
Passive — stop competitors from screwing up your tactics	Purpose	Active — win by screwing up competitors' tactics
Designed to maintain competitive advantage	Relationship to Competitive Advantage	A competitive advantage in and of itself

Figure 2.1. Differences between strategy and tactics

Strategy	Component	Tactics
General	**Specific or General**	Specific
Long-term	**Time Frame**	Short-term
Ordinary, general, mundane	**Unique or Ordinary**	Each tactic is unique
Not strategies	**Which Is Most Important in Winning Marketing Wars?**	Tactics are the most important elements in winning

Figure 2.1 (continued). Differences between strategy and tactics

- Make sure your plans are both flexible and adaptable to circumstances. The most common case in warfare is partial success, not total failure or total success. This means you need to have contingency plans for following up the result of your present campaign.

- Don't strike while your enemy is on guard. Why not? Because they're well placed to block or avoid your strike. Unless you're up against a very inferior opponent, no effective strike is possible until your enemy's power to resist or evade is paralyzed. This means your enemy is not only disorganized, but also demoralized. Your marketing intelligence can give you this information.

- Don't renew your attack along the same line after it has failed once before. If you only reinforce your position, it's also probable your enemy has reinforced his or her position in the same interval. Furthermore, the enemy has probably gained moral strength from their previous success in repulsing your attack.

The U.S. Army's Nine Principles of Warfare

- *Objective.* Every military operation should be directed towards a clearly defined, decisive, and attainable objective.

- *Offensive.* Seize, retain, and exploit the initiative.

- *Mass.* Concentrate combat power at the decisive place and time in order to achieve decisive results.

- *Economy of force.* Allocate minimum essential combat power to secondary efforts. This is a reciprocal of the principle of mass.

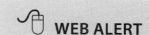 **WEB ALERT**

The U.S. Army's nine principles of warfare are taken from the U.S. Army Field Manual FM3-0, which is available free online: www.fas.org/irp/doddir/army/fm3-0.pdf.

- *Maneuver.* Place the enemy in a position of disadvantage through the flexible application of combat power. Be flexible, mobile, and maneuverable.

- *Unity of command.* Unify your effort under one responsible commander.

- *Security.* Good security keeps your enemy from getting an unexpected advantage.

- *Surprise.* Strike the enemy at a time and/or place and in a manner for which it is unprepared. This is the reciprocal of the principle of security.

- *Simplicity.* Prepare clear, uncomplicated plans and clear, concise orders to insure thorough understanding.

Remember: No single principle can be blindly adhered to — or observed — to the exclusion of the others. And no single principle can assure your victory in battle without reinforcement from one or more of the other principles.

3

Planning, War Games, and Winning Big

Planning sounds like a dry subject, doesn't it? War games sound like fun, don't they? But you can't play war games until you finish your planning, just like dessert doesn't come until you finish your meal. Many of you may be tempted to skip this chapter. But if you do, you won't become the 800-pound gorilla you want to be — or as I like to call the Business Warrior who wins big-time, the Big Dog. So before you skip over this chapter, look at these eleven basic steps to planning. Pick the one that interests you the most. Read it. Then go on to your second most interesting step. And so forth. I'll bet you finish reading the entire chapter!

1. Who should do the planning?
2. What should your business planning unit look like?
3. Understand your top management's objectives.
4. Analyze your situation.
5. Set objectives for each target market.
6. Develop and evaluate different strategies and tactics.
7. Calculate the risks.
8. Select your marketing strategies and tactics.
9. Determine your risk profile — falcon, sitting duck, chicken, or dodo bird.

10. Play war games.

11. Give your people their marching orders.

That's what you'll miss. So, make your decision — read it or go on to Chapter 4, "Winning the Battle for Your Customer's Mind."

Begin Here: Sun Tzu, Abe Lincoln, and Time Management Guru R. Alec Mackenzie

Want to hear what Sun Tzu said about losers? Here goes:

> The sure loser expects to win without planning, so he fights first without planning any strategy and tactics beforehand.

Was he talking about you? Or your competitor? And here's something Abraham Lincoln said:

> We must plan for the future because people who stay in the present will remain in the past.

Planning, indeed, *does* pay off — big-time! Research has consistently shown that companies that plan outperform those that don't in such measures of success as sales, earnings, profit, stock price, and growth rate.

Time management expert R. Alec Mackenzie said that although different types of managers engage in completely different operating activities (depending on their assignments within the company), they all engage in very similar managerial activities. Figure 3.1 shows what Mackenzie learned about how the nature of your job changes as you rise in management. Pay close attention to the percentages.

What does this chart tell you? Basically this — changes occur not only in the operating duties of the job, but also in the proportions of time spent in managing rather than in operating. Changes also occur in the five basic management functions: planning, organizing, staffing, directing, and controlling. Observe how the time required for planning increases — up to the point where it takes up 50 percent of the chief executive officer's time. Since it takes so little time of the people further down in the organization, these people don't pay very much attention to the importance of planning. When they move up in the organization, they often perform their much more important planning function poorly, basing their actions on their past casual learning experiences.

On the other hand, military personnel study planning at a very early stage in their careers. The military manager puts this study to use on a daily basis, for he or she is given much responsibility and authority in

Time Spent Managing or Delegating Planning, organizing, staffing, directing, controlling	Job	Time Spent Operating or Doing
30% Mostly directing, controlling (about 5% planning)	First-line supervisor, production	70%
50% Equally divided between planning, organizing, staffing, directing, controlling (about 10% planning)	Middle manager, personnel administration	50%
70% Mostly planning (25%), controlling (25%)	Top manager, marketing	30%
90% Mostly planning (50%)	Chief executive officer	10%

Figure 3.1. The nature of your job changes as you rise in management

this area very, very early. And so the military executive is generally more expert in planning than civilian business executives are. If your company is headed by a retired military man or woman, your planning is probably pretty good.

Now let's see what civilians can learn from military planning and how you can apply these lessons to your marketplace. First, we'll talk about decision making. Then, we'll go through the 11 planning steps I told you about at the beginning of this chapter.

Planning and Decision Making

Planning *is* decision making — making decisions about the future. The strategic marketing plan you develop is a set of action guidelines, and so it should be the responsibility of your company's operating executives, not your planning staff. Get involved with the plan yourself if you're an operating executive.

Procrastination

Some people find it hard to make decisions, though. They procrastinate. What about you? If you answer all or most of the following questions with *yes*, then you probably have a problem deciding:

- Do you try to invent excuses for not acting?
- Do you avoid getting one assignment ahead on repetitive assignments?
- Do you tend to OK half-measures so that you can avoid unpleasant action?
- Do you tend to avoid straightforward answers when you're pressed for a decision?
- Have you neglected the follow-up aspect of your action plans?
- Have you put off action because of fatigue or other physical factors?

People usually procrastinate on decision making to escape an overwhelming or unpleasant task, to excuse poor work, to gain sympathy, to get somebody else to do the job, to protect a weak self-image, or to avoid change. They do it by not setting deadlines, by over-committing themselves to too many projects, and so on. Procrastination, however, is self-defeating because it leads to:

- A waste of the present
- An unfulfilled life
- The anxiety of working under pressure
- The constant plague of unsolved problems
- Continuous frustration
- A life of indecision
- Boredom
- Fatigue
- Poor interpersonal relationships
- A mediocre career

Ulcer-less Decision Making

One of the highlights of my *Time Management* and *How To Be a Better Executive* seminars is this set of ten rules for ulcer-less decision making.

Follow them. They will help you make the right decision without procrastinating so much.

- Differentiate between big decisions and little problems. Most of your decision making will involve little problems, so spend as little time as possible worrying about them. Concentrate on the big decisions.

- Rely upon established policy whenever possible. That way, the only decision you have to make is simple: Should I or shouldn't I rely upon policy? You can even delegate this to your subordinates, who will come to you for advice only when they're uncertain.

- Consult and check with others who have expertise in the problem area. Don't rely upon yourself 100 percent here. If experts are available, use them.

- Avoid crisis decisions. Deciding under stress is far from ideal, and whatever the decision, the result is usually not a happy one.

- Don't try to anticipate all eventualities. You can't. Ask yourself what the odds are that something will go wrong. If the odds are low, don't worry about it. But be sure your odds are correct odds.

- Don't expect to be right all the time. Everybody is wrong some of the time. Remember, the results of making a poor decision are seldom as grim as the results of making a wrong decision. Once you realize that rightness is more a question of degree than perfection, it will be a lot easier for you to make decisions.

- Cultivate decisiveness. Get in the habit of making decisions and sticking to them.

- Once you make the decision, implement it right away. If you wait to implement it, chances are you will change your mind.

- Work on the hard decisions first, then the easy ones. If you put off the hard decisions until last, chances are you'll procrastinate and never make them.

- Make your decisions mathematically, if you're so inclined. I'll explain this later in this chapter in Step 8.

Now, let's review the 11 steps of the planning process itself.

STEP 1: Who Should Do the Planning?

Look again at Figure 3.1 at the beginning of this chapter. Time spent planning ranges from 5 percent at the lowest level to 50 percent at the CEO level.

STEP 2: What Should Your Business Planning Unit Look Like?

Each planning unit should consist of a specific product, product line, or mix of products that:

- Serves the same or a closely-related target market
- Shares common marketing program components, such as sales force, advertising, channels of distribution, and the like
- Is large enough to represent a meaningful unit in formulating strategy and in evaluating performance
- Is small enough to facilitate management and planning

STEP 3: Understand Your Top Management's Objectives

Before you can begin to work on your strategic marketing plan, you should understand clearly what top management's objectives and plans are for your section of the business. You'll need two kinds of information from people at the top:

1. The broad strategy your business unit is expected to pursue, and the financial resources that will be made available to you to carry out that strategy.

2. The specific expectations regarding sales, market share, and profit contribution. Figure 3.2 shows how these inputs affect the marketing tactics.

STEP 4: Analyze Your Situation ("So What?" Analysis, Not SWAT Analysis)

Military people are experts at situation analysis. At some companies, situation analysis is a very complicated process. At others, it's pretty

Tactics Involving:	Strategy 1: Invest for future growth.	Strategy 2: Target high-return/ high-growth segments and protect existing brand franchises.	Strategy 3: Manage for immediate cash flow.
Market share	Aggressively build across all segments.	Target high-return/ high-growth segments. Protect existing franchises.	Trade-off market share development for improved profits.
Pricing	Lower prices to build market share.	Stabilize prices for maximum profit contribution.	Raise prices, even at the expense of sales volume.
Promotion	Invest heavily to build market share.	Invest as the market dictates.	Engage in very little promotion.
Existing product line	Expand volume. Add line extensions to fill out product categories.	Shift product mix to higher profit products.	Eliminate low-contribution products and varieties.
New products	Expand product line by acquisition, self-manufacture, or joint venture.	Add products selectively and in controlled stages of commitment.	Add only certain winners.

Figure 3.2. How the marketing strategy you pick affects your tactics

simple. I prefer the simple approach. All you have to do is ask yourself which factors have an actual (or potential) impact on your company's ability to achieve your objectives. For each factor you think is important, ask "What difference does this make if it happens?" In other words, "So what?" If the difference really is important, then it's a significant factor, and you should pay close attention to it. Each significant factor will lead you to an opportunity, challenge, or new insight.

The six steps in situation analysis that I recommend here are based on several military situation analyses I've seen:

1. Collect information.

2. Ask yourself the question, "What business am I really in?"

3. Use *gap analysis* to select your *hit list* (target markets).

4. Analyze your final customers.

5. Analyze your distributors.

6. Analyze your competitors.

Let's examine each of these in turn.

Collect Information

There are a lot of good marketing research books out there as well as seminars on the subject. You can find out there in detail how to collect information. Right now, though, here are a few ethical, common-sense methods of collecting important information:

- Go to trade shows. Get stuff from your competitors' booths.

- Attend an evening MBA course. Network. Find out which firms the students work for. Term papers for these courses are often based on current projects at their companies.

- Massage your competitors' egos — treat them like experts. That will loosen their lips.

- Join a trade association.

- Hire a good market research firm.

 WEB ALERT

For more information on how to collect information go to GuerrillaDon.com. You can download an 8,000-word report that tells you how intelligence agencies such as the United States' CIA, Russia's KGB, United Kingdom's MI-6, and Israel's Mossad gather intelligence. The report shows you how to apply their techniques to collecting information about your customers and competitors. You'll read about espionage, spying, sabotage, and psychological warfare.

Ask Yourself "What Business Am I Really In?"

What's the first thing that comes to your mind when I say Xerox Corporation? Photocopying, right? Even though Xerox makes other products, let's stick with photocopying. So assume you work for Xerox's Printers Division. If I ask you who your competitors are, what would you say? If you're like most people, you'll first mention companies such as HP, Lexmark, Canon, and Epson. This is called *just plain competition*. But if you broaden your thinking (and you'll see how to do that in Chapter 5), you'll realize that there are many other competitors besides these businesses. Can you think of specific versions of the products Xerox makes that are in competition with one another? What about offset printing? This is called *product type competition*. If you broaden your thinking more, you'll realize competition also comes from other product categories that might satisfy the same consumer need such as word processors, apps, faxes, movies, computers, photography, and TV. This kind of *generic competition* is always around, whether or not there are active competitors offering the same product.

If you concentrate on *just plain competition,* you're ignoring many other real — and important — competitors. In a sense, you're thinking that your business is a rather limited one. But it's probably much bigger. If you remove your blinders and think in broader terms, you'll lose your *marketing myopia.*

It's dangerous to be myopic, or shortsighted, in a marketing sense. For example, around the beginning of the 20th century, if you owned shares of stock in railroads you were sitting pretty. Railroads were the largest, most profitable businesses in the United States. What happened to them? Most went bankrupt. That's because they myopically defined their business as the "railroad business." So they stayed on that narrow track. If they had thought of themselves as being in the "transportation business," they probably would still be the biggest businesses in the United States, because they would have gone into the automobile manufacturing business, made trucks, gone into the airplane business (manufacturing and transit), and so on. They would have been huge conglomerates today, and your stocks would have been worth much more.

Now let's look at an industry we all know and love that was myopic in a marketing sense before it took off its horse blinders: the motion picture industry. When television first became popular in the early-to-middle 1950s in the United States, movie executives got scared. They noticed drop-offs in movie attendance and attributed this to the free, in-home entertainment offered by television. They retaliated with a lousy promotional campaign proclaiming "Movies are better than ever." They refused to make TV series or even to sell old movies to TV networks and stations. But this didn't work. Attendance at movies continued to decline, even as TV ratings went up.

Eventually Warner Brothers executives decided they weren't in the movie business; they were in the entertainment business. In the late 1950s they made *Warner Brothers Presents* for ABC-TV. That opened the floodgates. Instead of fighting the competition, the movies preempted the competition. The movie industry removed its blinders, redefined its business more broadly, and eventually branched out into other fields of entertainment. Today, Universal Studios is part of NBC Universal Media (owned by Comcast), which owns amusement parks, television stations, and the like. Time Warner owns book publishers, record companies, and other entertainment businesses. If these other motion picture studios had remained in the narrowly defined movie business, they would be much smaller today, and some of them would no longer be in business at all.

What you should do is have a brainstorming session to define what business you're really in. This will help keep you from overlooking what may be several important competitors. See Chapter 5 for details on this and other ways to improve your creativity.

Use Gap Analysis to Select Your Hit List (Target Markets)

Look for a gap in the product and service offerings of the firms in the industry you're interested in. If you feel you can fill this gap profitably, go into it. Other important gaps to look for include:

- Bad debt rates that are too high
- Unsatisfied customer needs
- Geographic areas that are too remote
- Accounts that are too small (individual order size, total volume, or both)
- Quality requirements that are too high
- Service requirements that are too complex
- Price requirements that are too low
- Channels of distribution your competitors don't use

Electric Shock Therapy Down Under

I gave a talk to a group of executives in the electricity supply industry in Australia. At the cocktail party the night before my presentation, I overheard several executives talking. They were candid because they didn't know who I was. They kept wondering why the trade association hired somebody to talk to them about marketing, of all things! They didn't need marketing, they said. After all, there is no substitute for electricity. They were a monopoly.

Forewarned is forearmed. At the beginning of the talk the next day, I gave examples from the railroad and movie industries and told them they should broaden their thinking. I told them they had more competitors than they thought they did. Their biggest competition was leisure-time activities that take the family outside the home, such as automobile rides, picnics, hiking, and so on. When no one is home, home electricity usage falls dramatically.

I also told them about another competitor that they couldn't do anything about: Making love! It's usually done with the lights out — or dimmed. When people are making love, they use less electricity.

Finally, I told them they actually use marketing techniques to "de-market" electricity. In an era of scarce resources, many firms are trying to get their customers to cut back their power consumption, and several public utilities in the United States have run ads showing their customers how to save on electricity bills.

Can you fill any of these gaps at a profit? If you can, these are your potential target markets, the gaps you may want to fill with your products or services. Go after these target markets — put them on your hit list.

Analyze Your Final Customers

You'll read about this very complicated subject in Chapter 4, "Winning the Battle for Your Customer's Mind," in great detail.

Analyze Your Distributors

To reach your final customers you need the right distributors. How should you evaluate the different distributors you consider? Generally speaking, you should look at their financial well-being, territorial coverage, product line carried, sales strength, physical distribution capabilities, and managerial strength.

Analyze Your Competitors

In analyzing your competitors you need to:

1. Examine yourself first. Look carefully at the competitive price, service, selling effort, and advertising for each product line you have.

2. Then examine your key competitors. Figure out where they're vulnerable to the strategies you come up with. Find out why. Brainstorm what their reactions may be to your attempts to take market share away from them.

3. Figure out what strategies will give you the biggest market share gains. Do this for each of your competitors.

 WEB ALERT

GuerrillaDon.com has a checklist dealing with analysis of your competitors. Why not try it out now? Answer the questions and print it out. Then cover up the right-hand section of the figure. That's called "Comments made on the data." Also cover up the very bottom part of the figure. It's called "Key strategic conclusions." Write down your comments and conclusions and then see if they match the printed remarks. If they do, you're very good at what you do.

STEP 5: Set Objectives for Each Target Market

Remember reading Step 3? It wasn't that long ago (page 40). In that step you got the information you needed to understand your top management's objectives and plans for your section of the business. You may not have agreed with them, and you may have even argued against them. But eventually you agreed to abide by them. Gotta do what the bosses say, right? Well, now you're liberated. In Step 5 you're free to set your own objectives for each target market.

I can't tell you here which objectives you should set for each target market. That would require detailed knowledge of your specific situation. Over the years you've been exposed to many marketing objectives. You came up with the objectives yourself or your bosses gave them to you. Think about them as you read these 11 general guidelines for developing good marketing objectives. They've helped many of my clients over the years:

- *Use Benchmarks.* Use general descriptions only to establish benchmarks for change. Be extremely specific the rest of the time.

- *Use Numbers.* Put numbers on your objectives to make sure they're very specific. If you can't measure the progress you're making against your objectives, you can't control things. And if you can't count or measure them, you probably don't know what you want, and you should forget about them as goals.

- *Don't Use Numbers.* On the other hand, sometimes you can't be that specific. You may not have raw data available. When this happens, try to state your objectives in terms of gains, risks, expected values, utility, etc. — anything that tells you how effective your action has been.

- *Focus on Results.* Objectives should focus on results, not activity. For example, don't say you want to open five new accounts each month. It isn't the number of accounts opened that's important — it's the results obtained from those accounts that's important. Instead, say you want "to obtain $100,000 in extra profit by opening five new accounts each month." That will make you work harder to achieve your objective.

- *Understand.* Make sure everybody in your company understands the objectives.

- *Accept.* Make sure everybody accepts them, too.

- *Motivate.* Make sure everybody is motivated by them, too — your goals should be high, yet realistic. Sure, some reaching is necessary, but if you feel you can't accomplish a goal because it's too far out-of-line, then you won't even be motivated enough to try.

- *Overlook nothing.* Make sure you consider all constraints, including legal, environmental, and competitive. Don't overlook your financial limits, either.

- *Rank.* Rank your objectives from most important to least important. That way you're following what many experts have called the exception principle. You're concentrating on bringing the lagging area up to standard, not on the areas that are performing well already.

- *Be Flexible.* But be flexible in ranking. Two main reasons: First, you may have to give up objective A in order to get objective B. Second, you have to revise your objectives regularly. New opportunities, past failures, unanticipated events, and other changes are always happening, which means if you're inflexible, you lose.

- *Use MBO.* Finally, don't forget about using MBO, or management by objectives. You've heard of this all your business life. Get the people who are involved in carrying out the objectives to participate in setting them. That will make your objectives more realistic and will make people more committed to them.

The late George Odiorne made a ton of money when he came up with MBO. He struck a responsive chord in business executives all over the world — they were tired of having their bosses jam their ideas down their throats. How about your bosses? Do they let you participate? Or do they like to play emperor-for-life?

STEP 6: Develop and Evaluate Different Strategies and Tactics

You've already read about this in Chapter 2. Go back to it and pick out what you think is most important to you when you plan. If you're like me, you'll come to realize that Chapter 2 will help you prepare for counter-punches from your competitors.

STEP 7: Calculate the Risks

Try to calculate the risks involved in adopting different marketing strategies and tactics. Then select the specific strategies and tactics you'll use. Only then will you understand your risk profile (Step 9).

Earlier in this chapter, in the section on Planning and Decsion Making, we talked about how to make decisions without ulcers. There I said we'd talk about a mathematical approach to decision making later in the chapter. Well, here is it. It's all about risk-taking. It'll be fun to discover your risk profile: whether you're a falcon, a sitting duck, a chicken, or a dodo bird.

Risks and Decision Making

Everything you do in both your business and personal life involves some risk. Even crossing the street involves risk. Before crossing the street, we mentally assign a probability of reaching the other side alive. If the probability is high, we walk across. If it's low, we wait until the probability becomes high. We assess the probability of rain every morning so we'll know whether to carry an umbrella to work or not. We don't consciously think about these simple things in mathematical terms, but subconsciously that's what we do.

Business executives also assign probabilities on what the future holds in store. When you plan, you use your intuition to predict the results of your plans. And you choose one plan over another because you have given one of them a higher probability of success. If you're right in your probability assessments more often than you're wrong, you'll continue to be promoted and be successful in business. If you're wrong more often than you're right, you won't move up — and you might even get fired. Therefore, the better executives have a pretty good track record in predicting the future.

That's why you should believe you can predict the future to some degree. If you don't believe this, then skip over this section. It will be meaningless to you. On the other hand, you might learn something important — important enough to impress your boss and get you a raise and a promotion. Am I tempting you enough to make you keep on reading?

Calculate the Risks

Let's assume you have a decision to make. Your packaging specialist has designed a new label for your product. You have to choose between two courses of action open to you:

- Go with the new label. This is Action 1.

- Keep the old label. This is Action 2.

Only two things can possibly happen in the future. First, the new label will be better, or second, the old label will be better. You'll have to go with one of those two assumptions. To formalize your decision making process, draw a diagram like this:

Courses of Action You Can Choose	Assumption 1: New label is better	Assumption 2: Old label is better
Action 1: Go with new label		
Action 2: Stay with old label		

If you assume that the new label will be better in the future, what results will you expect if you take Action 1? Action 2? What if you assume the old label will be better?

Now, since you're an experienced business executive with a good track record, go ahead and put numbers into the two blank boxes. If you think you'll gain $10 million if you choose the new label and the new label is better, and if you think that you'll lose $5 million if you choose the new label and the old label is better, then put a plus 10 and minus 5 in the two blank boxes on the first row. If you think you'll gain $2 million if you choose the old label and the old label is better, and if you think that you'll lose $1 million if you choose the old label and the new label is better, then put minus 1 and plus 2 in the two blank boxes on the second row.

I've done this for you below.

Courses of Action You Can Choose	Assumption 1: New label is better	Assumption 2: Old label is better
Action 1: Go with new label	+ 10	− 5
Action 2: Stay with old label	− 1	+ 2

Warning: If you don't think you can do this with any accuracy, you probably shouldn't read this book, because you're probably too timid to advance very far in your organization.

Now, without looking ahead in this chapter, can you tell me what you would do? Would you choose the new label or stick with the old label? Think about it before answering.

After you make up your mind, read on.

STEP 8: Select Your Marketing Strategies and Tactics

Which alternative — which marketing strategy or tactic — did you choose? Much would depend on whether you're an optimist or a pessimist. In my seminars, I hold up half a glass of water and ask the participants to describe it. Eventually, somebody says it's *half full* and somebody says it's *half empty*. An optimist will say *half full,* and a pessimist will say *half empty.* (Paranoid nerds will worry that I'll spill the water on them. Cynical people will think there's gin in the glass, not water.)

I think most marketing executives are natural optimists, or they wouldn't be in such a stressful occupation. Let's look at the marketing action most optimists would choose — they'd go with the new label. Let's call this the *criterion of optimism.*

The criterion of optimism — maximize the maximum payoff. What's the maximum payoff associated with Action 1, going with the new label? Is it plus 10 or minus 5? It's plus 10, of course. What's the maximum payoff associated with Action 2, staying with the old label? Is it minus 1 or plus 2? It's plus 2, of course. So, I put these numbers in the table below. And since you're an optimist, you're going to maximize the maximum payoff. Which is maximum payoff? Is it plus 10 or plus 2? It's plus 10, because it's better to make $10 million than to make $2 million. And which action is associated with a maximum payoff of $10 million? It's Action 1. Therefore, go with the new label.

Courses of Action You Can Choose	Maximum Payoff
Action 1: Go with new label	+ 10
Action 2: Stay with old label	+ 2

The criterion of pessimism — maximize the minimum payoff. Now, let's say you're a pessimist. Pessimists follow this rule of thumb: Maximize the minimum payoff. Unlike optimists, who look at the most they can gain, pessimists look at the most they can lose. Look at Step 7 again and tell me the minimum payoff associated with Action 1 (new label). Is it plus 10 or minus 5? It's minus 5, of course. And what's the minimum payoff associated with Action 2 (old label)? Is it minus 1 or plus 2? It's minus 1, of course. I put those numbers in the table below. Since you're a pessimist now, you'll maximize the minimum payoff. Which is the minimum payoff? Is it minus 5 or minus 1? It's minus 1, because it's better to lose $1 million than to lose $5 million. Which action is associated with a minimum payoff of minus 1? It's Action 2. Therefore, stay with the old label.

Courses of Action You Can Choose	Minimum Payoff
Action 1: Go with new label	– 5
Action 2: Stay with old label	– 1

But neither the criterion used by the optimist nor the criterion used by the pessimist is really good enough to help you make good decisions. What happens in the real world doesn't depend on whether you're an optimist or a pessimist. To make this exercise more meaningful, you've got to assign mathematical probabilities to your Assumption 1 occurring or to your Assumption 2 occurring instead. How can you do this?

What do you do when you're flipping coins? You have no idea if heads or tails will come up, so you assign a 50 percent probability to heads and a 50 percent probability to tails. In the real world, if you have no idea whether the new label or the old label is better, then you should assign a 50-50 probability to each, just as you do when flipping coins. Once you assign the 50-50 probability, then you multiply your original numbers by the 50-50 probabilities and add them up across algebraically, just as you did back in high school. This is shown below.

Courses of Action You Can Choose	50-50 Probability Calculation	Payoff
Action 1: Go with new label	+10 (Assumption 1) times 0.5 (50% probability) minus 5 (Assumption 2) times 0.5 (50% probability)	+ 2.5
Action 2: Stay with old label	- 1 (Assumption 1) times 0.5 (50% probability) plus 2 (Assumption 2) times 0.5 (50% probability)	+ 0.5

The end result of Action 1 (new label) is a gain of $2.5 million, and the end result of Action 2 (old label) is a gain of $500,000. Now, no matter if you're an optimist or a pessimist, which act will you choose? It's better to gain $2.5 million than $500,000, so you choose Action 1 — choosing the new label.

But you can do better than that. Assigning a 50-50 probability is for kids. You, as a good marketing executive, probably had some good market research done for you. This means you can now assess a more realistic probability on whether the new or old label is better.

Let's say your market research tells you the new label is probably better, so you assign a 70 percent probability to Assumption 1 (new label is better). That means you have to assign a 30 percent probability to Assumption 2 (old label is better). This is because the two probabilities have to add up to 100 percent. This is shown below.

Courses of Action You Can Choose	70-30 Probability Calculation	Payoff
Action 1: Go with new label	+ 10 (Assumption 1) times 0.7 (70% probability) minus 5 (Assumption 2) times 0.3 (30% probability)	+ 5.5
Action 2: Stay with old label	- 1 (Assumption 1) times 0.7 (70% probability) plus 2 (Assumption 2) times 0.3 (30% probability)	- 0.1

If you take Action 1 (go with new label), you'll gain $5.5 million. If you take Action 2 (stay with old label), you'll lose $100,000. Naturally, you'll choose to go with the new label, Action 1.

On the other hand, let's say market research tells you the old label is probably much better than the new label. You assign a 90 percent probability to Assumption 2 (old label is better), and a 10 percent probability to Assumption 1 (new label is better). This is shown below.

Courses of Action You Can Choose	10-90 Probability Calculation	Payoff
Action 1: Go with new label	+ 10 (Assumption 1) times .1 (10% probability) minus 5 (Assumption 2) times .9 (90% probability)	- 3.5
Action 2: Stay with old label	- 1 (Assumption 1) times .1 (10% probability) plus 2 (Assumption 2) times .9 (90% probability)	+ 1.7

If you take Action 2 (stay with old label), you'll gain $1.7 million. If you take Action 2 (go with new label), you'll lose $3.5 million. Naturally, you'll stay with the old label.

See how it works? To make sure you do, make the arithmetic calculations I just did. If you do the math, you'll remember this process much better than if you just glance at it.

STEP 9: Determine Your Risk Profile

Look at Figure 3.3, the risk profile grid. To determine your risk profile you need to mark three spots on the grid.

On the horizontal axis, you assess the probability of an event occurring, as you did earlier, and so you place your X somewhere between 0 and 100. You also make a judgment about how much money you'll win or lose, just as you did earlier. Put an X on the top left-hand axis next to the amount of money you think you'll gain, and put an X on the bottom right-hand axis next to the amount of money you think you'll lose. Then join the top left X and the middle X with a line, and join the middle X and the bottom right X with another line. Now you've got your risk profile. But what does it mean? Take a look at Figure 3.4. This shows you four risk profiles, all named after birds because they look like the wings of birds in flight. I call them the *falcon*, the *chicken*, the *sitting duck*, and the *dodo bird*. Which of the four risk profiles does yours resemble?

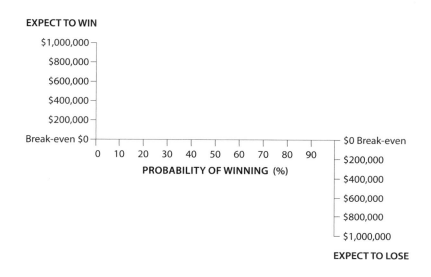

EXPECT TO WIN

Figure 3.3. Create your risk profile

The falcon flies high and fast, and swoops down low to attack its prey. This is a rather risky way to maneuver, but the successful falcon eats a lot when it kills its prey. If it misses, though, the bird might crash into the ground and injure itself severely. If you feel you have much to gain and much to lose, you're probably a falcon.

Whether you should adopt this risk strategy or not depends on where you place the X on the horizontal axis — what the probability of winning or losing is. In the falcon example in Figure 3.4, I assessed the probability of winning at 65 percent and the probability of losing at 35 percent. If you feel comfortable with these probabilities, then adopt this strategy.

If you're a military buff like me, you'll like this story: General Douglas MacArthur was a falcon at the Inchon landing in Korea in 1951. He took a high risk to surprise the North Koreans. Around Inchon high tides occur about six hours each month, and these high tides are necessary to make an amphibious landing. The North Koreans, never suspecting their enemies would land there, had most of their troops elsewhere, and so MacArthur was able to cut their lines of communication. He began a pincer movement, which eventually destroyed the enemy and drove the North Koreans back to the Chinese border in a few short months. MacArthur knew the risks were high, but he also knew he could win big

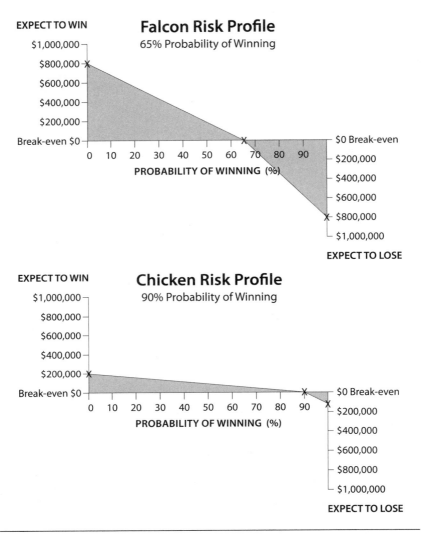

Figure 3.4. The four risk profiles: falcon, chicken, sitting duck, and dodo bird

if he were successful. And his sufficient planning cut his risk down to a manageable size — and so he won.

Many business executives adopt the chicken risk profile. If you're a chicken the probability of winning is quite high. In the example shown in Figure 3.4, it's 90 percent. However, the potential gain is relatively small, as is the amount of potential loss. Many cautious executives like this profile best. How about you? Are you cautious or a little reckless?

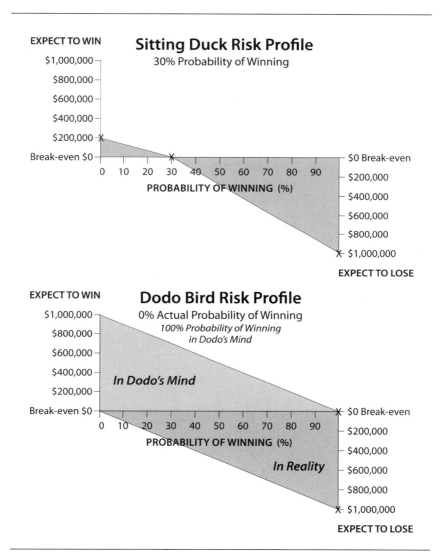

Figure 3.4 (continued). The four risk profiles

Business executives who adopt the sitting duck risk profile, where the probability of winning is quite low (30 percent in Figure 3.4), are just plain stupid. There the amount of potential gain is small, and the potential loss is quite large.

And anybody who adopts the dodo bird risk profile is long gone — zero probability of winning. This happens to many inexperienced business executives. They're overly optimistic, and so they assess their probabilities without much serious thought or market research. They think their new venture is a sure thing, that even if they do badly, they'll still make a little, and if they do well they'll make a lot. But instead, they'll lose everything

I hope you're not that naïve. There are very few sure things in the business world. Winning is hard, and naïve executives soon become as extinct as the dodo.

STEP 10: Play War Games

Try Out Your Strategies and Tactics in Business Simulations

There are many computer-based business simulations. Here's your lucky thirteen list of some of the best business war games I could find for you to check out. First, ten from the United States:

- Blueline Simulations. BluelineSims.com
- BTS. BTS.com
- BusSim Business Simulations. Bussim.info
- Capsim Business Simulations. Capsim.com
- Executive Perspectives. epsims.com
- Forio Business Simulations. Forio.com
- Income/Outcome. Income-Outcome.com (see box to the right)
- Insight Experience. Insight-Experience.com
- Marketplace Business Simulations. Marketplace-Simulation.com
- Tycoon Systems. IndustryMasters.com

Next, two from the United Kingdom:

- Hall Marketing. Simulations.co.uk
- Profitability Business Simulations. Profitability.com/uk

Finally, a Finland-based company with branches all over the world:

- Cesim. Cesim.com

Before you contact these companies, though, please look at the end of Chapter 10 where you'll be introduced to an in-basket war game (The Business Warrior Worksheet) that will tie together everything you learned about the four Ps of the marketing mix. It begins on page 176.

The Income-Outcome Game

Here's some information about the Income-Outcome game, which is conducted in a classroom situation — without dice, chance cards, or spinners.

In its simulation, players become entrepreneurial executives, their teams become corporate giants (or fail), and the classroom becomes an entire industry. The simulation rewards change and innovation and shows how a competitive market will push companies to reduce prices and improve.

Each team of Business Warriors sits at its own table and plots strategy and tactics. Each has its own board, which shows all the line items of the team's financial statements. It gives them a battlefield view of their cost structure, cash flow situation, inventory levels, borrowing power, etc.

All the information is available to everyone. As in chess, winning depends on how the team can plan into the future, how well it can anticipate its competitors' moves, how much flexibility it can keep, and how well it can respond to its opponent's unexpected moves and situations — good or bad, intentional or accidental.

Teamwork is critical. A team that has difficulty sharing ideas, getting and analyzing information, or making decisions in a timely fashion will end up with lousy financial results.

It's not a zero-sum game. Usually the winners are the teams who have made the most money. But in a bitterly contested and badly managed session, the winners could be the team that has lost the least amount.

Try Out Your Strategies and Tactics in a Few Test Markets

Your company uses certain cities over and over for its test marketing. If they work, keep on using them. If you're starting from scratch, though, here are six useful guidelines:

Two dos:

- Make sure the test market demographics reflect those of your overall target market.

- Your test market should be a self-contained market, without any dependence on a neighboring area. This avoids media spillover and buying from wholesalers outside the market area.

Three don'ts:

- The test market shouldn't be over-tested.

- It shouldn't be dominated by any one industry, nationality, or racial group, nor should it have high unemployment or seasonal layoffs.

- It shouldn't have an unusual historical development in your product category.

One more guideline:

- The test market shouldn't be too big or too small. Many U.S. companies like to use cities with populations between 75,000 and 300,000.

Of course, once your competitors know you're in a test market, they'll do things to screw you up — extra heavy media buys, special deals, etc. Some firms use laboratory stores, but I don't recommend that option. Contact me at Donald_Hendon@hotmail.com, and I'll tell you why.

STEP 11: Give Your People Their Marching Orders

In the military, an *operations order* formally assigns the responsibility and authority necessary to accomplish the objective you've set to the people who will carry out that process. The same thing happens in the business world. *Marching orders* are given to line and staff personnel in the company so that the plan is implemented correctly. What's in these marching orders?

- Directives on how to use the information gathered in three of the steps in the planning process — the results of your situation analysis (Step 4), the objectives you set for each target market (Step 5), and the specific marketing strategies and tactics you chose (Step 8).

- Plus two more directives — how to obtain the administrative and logistical support your plan needs and what controls will be necessary to monitor the progress of the operation.

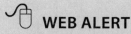

WEB ALERT

Go to GuerrillaDon.com to see an example of marketing marching orders for a large corporation. I like it for four reasons:

- I helped them write it when I was a consultant to the company.
- It's brief. It covers everything in these steps in only 960 words.
- Its objectives are very specific.
- It gives specific directions to people who will be implementing the plan.

When you write your marching orders, make sure you put these five directives in that precise order. Why? Because they logically follow one another.

Moving Forward: Your Plan of Action

Make no mistake about it, planning — good planning — is essential to your success, to your very survival as a company and as a business executive. Security analysts and institutional investors know this — they often insist on spending time with planners before they will recommend a company to their own clients.

But planning isn't enough. You've got to *implement* your plan. Here are five things I tell my clients to be concerned about if they want to be winning Business Warriors:

- Make sure all your key people are thoroughly knowledgeable about how to plan. In most companies this knowledge is unevenly distributed in the organization — some key people know how to plan, some don't.

- Make sure senior-level managers back up your planning efforts.

- Make sure both planning staff and line executives are involved in your planning process.

- Don't rush things. Don't allow management-by-crisis to take over your planning process. Most things done in a hurry are done poorly.

- KISS your plan. (Keep It Short and Simple. Some say Keep It Simple, Stupid!) Don't overcomplicate things. Add complexity very reluctantly and only when your company is ready for it. When in doubt, don't add complexity. Why invite trouble?

4

Winning the Battle for Your Customer's Mind

THE THREE Ps OF MARKETING

Most of you are familiar with *the four Ps of marketing* — price, product, promotion, and place. Right now, let's talk about a different set of Ps: *the three powers of marketing warfare* — personality, positioning, and psychographics. These three Ps deal with your customer's mind.

Mao Tse-Tung said "The fountainhead of warfare is in the masses of the people. And we must inspire them to cooperate voluntarily. We must not force them. If we try, it won't work."

This means that military warfare and business warfare are very much alike — both are a battle for the minds of people — Mao's masses and your customers. Using the three Ps of marketing warfare will help you win your battle for your customers' minds. After you digest this chapter, add these three Ps to your arsenal of weapons.

Personality

Brand personality is nothing more than describing your brand as if it were a human being. This is important because people favor products that match their own self-image or personality. For example, Emily may see herself as sophisticated and traditional, and she will favor a perfume that projects these same qualities. If Yves St. Laurent's Elle perfume is promoted as a perfume for sophisticated and traditional women, then its brand personality will match Emily's personality, and she is more likely to buy it.

Once you think you've got your brand's personality down on paper, have your ad agency make up an ad with the personality featured prominently in it. Pretest it and see what you have. The litmus test is to delete the name of your brand from the ad and see if respondents can tell you its name. If they can, you've got a pretty good brand personality, one that is readily identifiable.

For example, if you removed the Geico name from its insurance ads (but kept the lizard), most people would probably recognize it as a Geico ad. If you removed Ford's name from its service ads, most people probably wouldn't be able to recognize it as a Ford ad. Geico has a brand personality, but Ford doesn't.

Now, look at this list of ten brands. See if you can tell which brands have distinct personalities and which don't:

- *Cigarettes:* Marlboro or Winston?

- *Peanut butter:* Peter Pan or Jif?

- *Toilet paper:* Charmin or Scott Tissue?

- *Beverage mix:* Kool-Aid or Wyler's?

- *Portable media players:* Apple I-Pod or Zune?

If you're like me, you figured Marlboro, Peter Pan, Charmin, Kool-Aid, and Apple I-Pod have distinct brand personalities, and Winston, Scott Tissue, Wyler's, Jif, and Zune do not. Look at their ads and learn from them.

You can also learn from the famous motivation researcher Ernest Dichter. He said, "The objects which surround us have more than utilitarian properties — they serve as a kind of mirror which reflects our own image." Here are the personalities that fifteen products have, according to Dichter:

- *Your first automobile:* A puberty symbol, showing you can now get away from your parents for the first time and be on your own.

- *Beds:* The refuge, the womb to which you can return for security and protection.

- *Carpets:* Commitment and warmth. They pull the home together. The thicker the carpet, the more prestige.

- *Charity:* Allows us to play God, to be arrogant by giving.

- *Hot tea:* Feminine. Removes irritability and nervousness, cures colds.

- *Iced tea:* Removes vague and bottomless restlessness, restores psychic balance.

- *Ice cream:* Abundance, love, affection, effortless satisfaction.

- *Lipstick:* Warmth, generosity, friendliness, humor. Using it overcomes a woman's frustrations, but it's also a visible proof of a somewhat sinful relation.

- *Power tools:* Omnipotence.

- *Rum:* Masculine, strength, harshness, tropical.

- *Scotch:* Status, prestige, authentic not synthetic, stylish, no after-effects.

- *Skiing:* Flying with your own wing-like foot extensions. Potency — conquering the virgin snow. Snobbish superiority.

- *Soup:* The brew of the good fairy, with magic power to heal, protect, and give strength, courage, and the feeling of belonging.

- *Spaghetti:* Family fun, conviviality.

Positioning, Military Style

In the late 1960s and early 1970s, Al Ries and Jack Trout owned an ad agency in the rich Connecticut suburbs of New York City. It wasn't going anywhere. In 1972 the partners convinced *Advertising Age's* editor Jim O'Gara to run a series of three articles by them in three consecutive issues (April 24 – May 8, 1972). *Advertising Age* was then and still is one of the leading advertising and marketing trade journals in the United States, and it had (and still has) very desirable demographics. It continues to be a very influential publication today.

In their articles, essentially a rewrite of two articles they wrote in 1969 and 1971 for the much smaller trade journal *Industrial Marketing,* they coined a new term for a marketing technique that had been around for a long time under many different names, including segmentation, share-of-mind, and unique selling proposition (Rosser Reeves' famous USP).

Basically, they said that in order to stand out from competitors in an over-communicated world, ads must be very different. Well, that's what Rosser Reeves said, too, but Reeves was hard-sell. To be different from Reeves, they got rid of the hard-sell part and called their technique positioning, and they said a lot more about how to do it instead of simply saying "Be unique." They could have called it market segmentation of the customer's mind or USP minus the hard sell, but *positioning* was shorter and sounded better.

This name would have been the term for a short-lived fad except for one thing—they dared to predict which current ad campaigns would succeed (those with elements of positioning) and which ones would fail (those without positioning). They took a big chance. If they had made the wrong predictions their ad agency would probably have gone out of business shortly thereafter. But they were correct, and the old time-tested techniques continued to be widely used, but this time under the now-famous name positioning.

And the Trout-Ries agency prospered. And they both became very rich. And that's why you're reading about positioning today. It's really *that* important!

Well, that's the background. Now, here are the specifics:

The Importance of Being First

Positioning maintains that what is *most* important is how the brand is ranked in your customer's mind against your competition—much more important than your brand's features and images. Let's see why. Ask yourself these six questions:

- Who was the first person to fly solo across the North Atlantic Ocean?
- Who was the second?
- Who was the first person to walk on the moon?
- Who was the second?
- What is the highest mountain in the world?
- What is the second?

Most of you knew who or what was first but not second. The firsts were Charles Lindbergh, Neil Armstrong, and Mount Everest. The first person, the first company, the first brand to occupy any position in your prospect's mind is going to be very hard to dislodge—Xerox copiers,

Hertz car rentals, General Electric electricity, Coca-Cola cola drinks, and so forth — even though other brands may have higher market share.

Still skeptical? Here are two more questions that will get rid of your skepticism:

- Who is the first person you ever kissed?
- Who is the second?

Like a memory bank, the mind has slots or positions — one position for each piece of information it chooses to keep. But the mind is not a computer and can't save everything. In fact, we live in an over-communicated society where the annual per-capita consumption of advertising in the United States today is around $1,000. Let's say you spend $1 million a year on advertising. That may sound like a big amount, but you're really hitting the average customer with approximately one third of one cent of advertising, spread out over 365 days.

How will your ad message stand out and be kept in the customer's memory? Our minds reject most of the ad messages we're bombarded with. In general, our minds accept only new pieces of information that match our prior experience and knowledge. Just like the names of Lindbergh, Armstrong, Mount Everest, and your first lover are burned indelibly in your mind, so, too, is the first brand to occupy a position — any position — in your customer's mind. Thus, IBM, Xerox, Hertz, General Electric, and Coca-Cola have great advantages over Toshiba, Ricoh, National, Westinghouse, and Pepsi. For the number twos, the number threes, and the also-rans to obtain a favorable position in their buyers' minds, they must relate their brands in some way to the number-one brand's position.

Share-of-Mind

There's not much room for too many brands in the customer's mind, so marketers talk about share-of-mind. Market researchers ask people to name as many brands as they can think of in a certain product category. Most people will first name the brand they use, and follow that with just two other brands. Market shares correlate with share-of-mind, in most cases. If your share-of-mind is not in the top three, your market share is abysmally poor.

It's almost impossible to move your brand into the top three if your new brand is positioned against an old brand. Our minds have no room for the new and the different unless the new and the different are related to the old and familiar in some way. Positioning tells us that it's much better to tell your prospect what the brand is *not,* rather than what it *is.* For example, the first automobile was positioned as a *horseless carriage,* which allowed the prospect to think of the auto as it related to the primary existing mode of transportation, the horse.

Leaders

Now, if you're already number one, what can you do to keep on top? It's really much easier than you think: Coca-Cola couldn't put much of a dent into Dr Pepper's sales with its Mr. Pibb brand, and IBM couldn't do very much against Xerox in the photocopier field, even though Coke and IBM had much greater resources than did Dr Pepper and Xerox. Here are four hints on how to stay on top:

First. Don't run ads screaming "We're number one." Why not? Because either your prospect knows you're number one and wonders why you're so insecure or doesn't know you're number one and doesn't believe you. Why create doubt in somebody's mind?

Second. Reinforce the original concept instead. As Coca-Cola did, say your brand is "the real thing," instead of saying "We are number one." The real thing, like your first lover, will always occupy a special place in your prospect's mind.

Third. Cover all bets and buy out every new product development as soon as it shows some sign of promise. Here's a dumb mistake made by two huge companies: Kodak and 3M declined to cover their bets when they were offered buying rights to the xerography process. An unknown company named Haloid bought the rights — it's now known as Xerox. Remember this: Covering all bets sometimes means a multi-brand strategy or tactic. But make certain each of your new brands occupies a position *different* from your other brands, or your new brands will cannibalize your old brands. Instead of changing the favorable position Ivory bar soap had in the prospect's mind, Procter & Gamble brought out Tide when heavy-duty laundry detergents became available. And when dishwasher detergents became available, Procter & Gamble didn't mess with Tide's favorable position. Instead, it brought out Cascade.

Fourth. React quickly and viciously whenever competitors introduce radically new concepts. Strike fear into their hearts and minds. Let them know you're mean and nasty. General Foods introduced red-canned Horizon coffee in the east just before red-canned Folgers and red-canned Hills Brothers coffee moved into the east, where General Foods' blue-canned Maxwell House was (and still is) the number-one coffee.

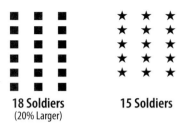

18 Soldiers
(20% Larger)

15 Soldiers

Figure 4.1. The Square Army versus the Star Army — *before* the battle

Trout and Ries said that General Foods was simply taking the advice of Clausewitz, who said Napoleon's objective in a battle was not merely to outmaneuver but to annihilate the opposing force. (Trout and Ries put it this way: Keep attacking until you hear from the U.S. Federal Trade Commission.)

"A suspension in the act of warfare contradicts the nature of war, because two armies are two incompatible elements, and they should destroy each other. Just like fire and water, they can never put themselves in equilibrium. Instead, they act and react upon one another until one disappears." (As Trout and Ries said: IBM takes no prisoners.)

"Pursuit is a second act of the victory, in many cases more important than the first." (Again from Trout and Ries: Too many companies quit when they're ahead.)

Followers

Positioning is especially suited to brands in the number two, three, four, or even worse positions. It's very dangerous to try to compete head-on against a company that has a strong number-one brand. Let's see how insights from military strategy and tactics can help you understand why attacking the leader head-on usually leads to disaster. Look at Figure 4.1.

Let's say you're the Square Army, and you have 18 soldiers. You're attacking the Star Army, which has 15 soldiers. Your army is 20 percent larger than theirs. Let's say that each army fires one bullet per soldier in a simultaneous volley and that every third bullet fired kills one enemy soldier. How many volleys will it take for your Square Army to annihilate the enemy Star Army? You'll need to use your pencil and paper to figure out this problem. Try to do it without looking at Figure 4.2, which gives you the answer. So don't read ahead.

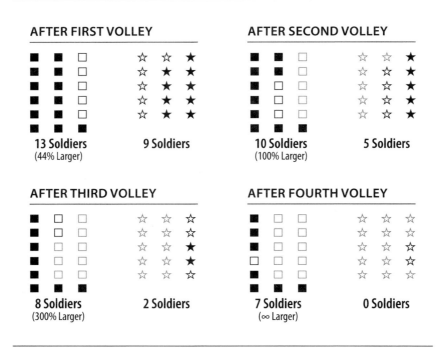

Figure 4.2. The Square Army versus the Star Army — *after* the battle

Now that you've finished, check Figure 4.2 for the answer.

- *At the beginning:* You have 18 soldiers, they have 15 — you're 20 percent larger.

- *After the first volley:* You have 13 soldiers, they have 9 — you're 44 percent larger.

- *After the second volley:* You have 10 soldiers, they have 5 — you're 100 percent larger.

- *After the third volley:* You have 8 soldiers, they have 2 — you're 300 percent larger.

- *After the fourth volley:* You have 7 soldiers, they have none — you've wiped them out.

So you came out victorious. OK, but how long did it take you? Four volleys. How expensive was it for you? First of all, time is money, and four volleys may have been too long for you. Second, you lost 11 soldiers — 61 percent of your original eighteen. That was a very costly head-to-head

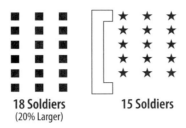

18 Soldiers
(20% Larger)

15 Soldiers

**Figure 4.3. The stronger Square Army versus the better-fortified Star Army
— *before* the battle**

attack, even though you had 20 percent more resources than your enemy did at the beginning.

Now, let's change the scenario a little. Let's say you still have eighteen soldiers, and they still have 15 soldiers, so once more you have a 20 percent advantage in resources. Now let's say they have a strongly entrenched position, but you don't. Notice the barrier in Figure 4.3.

In Business Warrior terms, the barrier means they have a number-one position in your prospects' minds, a strong brand, strong advertising, great distribution, and so forth. Once again, both armies are going to fire one bullet per soldier in simultaneous volleys. Your enemy, the Star Army, still kills one of you with every third bullet they fire, but since they now have such a strong defense, you can kill one of them only with every sixth bullet fired.

Now, get out your pencil and paper again and figure out who is going to win *this* head-to-head combat. Again, don't look at Figure 4.4 yet, which gives you the answer, and only read what comes next after you've figured out this problem.

Now that you've finished, check Figure 4.4 for the new answer.

- *At the beginning:* You have 18 soldiers, they have 15 — you're 20 percent larger.

- *After the first volley:* You have 13 soldiers, they have 12 — you're 8 percent larger.

- *After the second volley:* You have 9 soldiers, they have 10 — they're 11 percent larger.

- *After the third volley:* You have 6 soldiers, they have 8 — they're 33 percent larger.

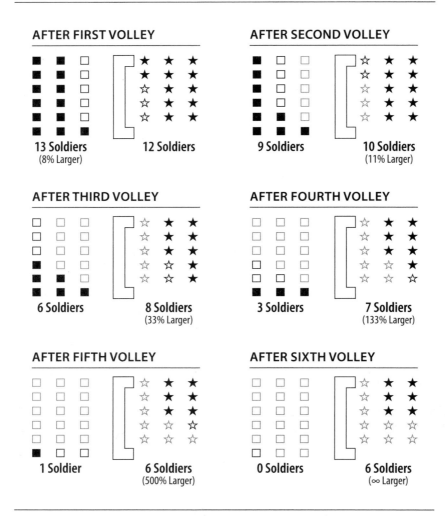

Figure 4.4. The stronger Square Army versus the better-fortified Star Army — *after* the Battle

- *After the fourth volley:* You have 3 soldiers, they have 7 — they're 133 percent larger.

- *After the fifth volley:* You have 1 soldier, they have 6 — they're 500 percent larger.

- *After the sixth volley:* You have no soldiers left, they have 6 — they've annihilated you this time!

The moral is that you'll need *tremendously great* superiority if you launch a frontal attack against a strongly entrenched competitor or you'll lose. Even if you have a decent competitive advantage, your resources will be bled from you: You lost 61 percent of your soldiers when you started off with a 20 percent advantage in resources in the first example.

What can you learn from this? Frontal attacks are the riskiest forms of warfare. Military strategists and tacticians say you need at least a three-to-one advantage in numbers or resources to be sure of victory without losing too much. Most companies don't have this advantage. And so this is why positioning is especially suited to followers. It opens up the possibility of attacking the frontrunner without serious loss and with a good chance of winning.

How to Turn Followers into Big Winners

What can a follower do to beat the Big Dog? First, try these tactics:

- Never use a me-too approach. Find a unique position to fill, such as:
    - By attributes (Crest is a cavity fighter)
    - By price/quality (Wal-Mart is a value store)
    - By competitor (Avis tries harder)
    - By application (Gatorade is for quick, healthful energy after exercise and other forms of physical exertion)
    - By product user (Miller is for blue-collar, heavy beer drinkers)
    - By product class (Carnation Instant Breakfast is a breakfast food)

- Create a better brand name. When Allegheny Airlines changed its name to USAir, people no longer regarded it as small and regional. But when Singer put its name on business machines, it lost $371 million because customers didn't transfer its brand name recognition to a different product sold to a different market.

- Launch your attack before the leader has time to establish leadership — if it's possible.

- Use a massive advertising and promotion campaign. Try for that three-to-one advantage.

- Do extensive market research to find the features your prospects want in your brand, and put as many of them as you can in your brand. Of course, it's not enough to just make a better product, which makes you focus on your features; you also have to focus on the benefits your prospects want.

- Do extensive market research.

- Read my book, *Guerrilla Deal-Making: How to Put the Big Dog on Your Leash and Keep Him There* (Morgan James, 2013). It's co-authored by Jay Conrad Levinson, the famous guerrilla marketing guru. You'll learn the 100 most powerful weapons guerrilla marketers use against Big Dogs.

The second thing you should do is ask yourself these six questions. They are simple to ask, but they're pretty hard to answer. Why? Because they raise issues that will test your courage and beliefs.

- What position do you own *now*? Do market research to find out.

- What position do you *want* to own? Make sure you choose a position that is profitable now and won't become obsolete in the future. (How many products named *Sputnik* or *Disco* are still around? Hell, how many of you even remember what a *Sputnik* is — or was? Google it and find out.)

- Who must you outfight? Select a *gap*, a position that nobody else has a firm grip on, so you'll be able to avoid a head-to-head confrontation with the market leaders. (You read about this in Chapter 3, pages 44 – 45.)

- Do you have enough money? In an over-communicated society, where a $1 million advertising budget translates into less than half of one cent per customer per day, and where a 30-second TV commercial on the Super Bowl in January 2013 cost around $3,800,000, you're going to have to spend heavily to get above the noise level. You may have to limit yourself to just a few geographic areas at first, and then roll out your program to other locations later.

- Can you stick it out? Positioning works best over a long period of time. The best positioning campaigns, including Marlboro (the cowboy), Crest (no cavities), McDonald's (Ronald McDonald), and others have been around for many years. However, expect internal pressure for change from people who want immediate results.

Activities	Interests	Opinions
• Work	• Family	• Themselves
• Hobbies	• Home	• Social Issues
• Social Events	• Job	• Politics
• Vacation	• Community	• Business
• Entertainment	• Recreation	• Economics
• Club Membership	• Fashion	• Education
• Community	• Food	• Products
• Shopping	• Media	• Future
• Sports	• Advertisements	• Culture

Figure 4.5. Lifestyles are expressed through activities, interests, and opinions

- Do all your marketing communications match your position? It's very important to make sure your entire marketing mix reinforces the position you've picked, or you'll confuse your prospects.

Psychographics

Psychographics is market segmentation of the mind. It's measuring people's lifestyles. Someone's life-style refers to their pattern of living as expressed by their activities, interests, and opinions — AIOs for short. Figure 4.5 shows you examples of AIOs.

To discover a person's psychographic profile, ask how strongly he or she agrees or disagrees with statements such as the following:

- My children are the most important thing in my life. (Child-oriented)

- My friends or neighbor often come to me for advice. (Self-designated opinion leader)

- Food should never be left in the refrigerator uncovered. (Wrapper)

- I like to try new and different things. (New brand trier)

To measure lifestyles/psychographics, you need a very long questionnaire — usually between 100 and 200 statements like the ones above. People can fill out the questionnaire fairly quickly, though, since a five-point scale (from strongly agree to strongly disagree) is used to measure their agreement with each statement, and it only takes a second for them to select one of the five choices. Market researchers then analyze the responses to the questionnaire and puts those responses into distinctive psychographic groups. For example, a national study of household food buying identified four psychographic segments:

- *Hedonists* (20 percent of the market) enjoy the good life and foods that taste good, are convenient, and inexpensive. They are most likely young, male, and childless. Example: Hardee's and Carl's Jr.

- *Don't wants* (20 percent) sacrifice taste, price, and convenience to obtain foods without sugar, artificial ingredients, cholesterol, and fats. They are older, better educated, live in large urban areas, and have no children at home. Example: Truvia.

- *Weight conscious* (33 percent) are primarily concerned about calories and fat, so they avoid cholesterol, sugar and salt, but they like convenience foods and don't avoid artificial ingredients. They are most likely women employed full time, with higher incomes. Example: Diet Coke.

- *Moderates* (25 percent) are average in almost everything, including consumption levels and demographics. They don't exhibit strong concerns about the avoidance factors and balance the tradeoffs they make in food selection.

In preparing your marketing plans for your brand, look for relationships between your brand and psychographic groups. Aim your brand at a relevant group; then your advertising copywriter can create advertising that matches the activities, interests and opinions in this group's lifestyle. In the food buying example above, depending on your brands, you could target the weight-conscious people with low-calorie products, or target the hedonists with delicious, fattening foods.

You can tell that psychographic profiles give you a much richer description of a potential market segment than using demographics alone. Using psychographics will help you make the right promotional decisions by matching your brand's image with the type of consumer who uses the product category. You can see this by looking at the profile of heavy users of eye makeup:

- *Demographic characteristics:* Young, well-educated, live in metropolitan areas

- *Product use:* Also heavy users of liquid face makeup, lipstick, hair spray, perfume, cigarettes, gasoline

- *Media preferences:* Fashion magazines, *The Tonight Show,* adventure programs

- *Activities, interests, and opinions (Psychographics):* Agree more than average with these statements:
  - I often try the latest hairdo styles when they change.
  - An important part of my life and activities is dressing smartly.
  - I like to feel attractive to all men.
  - I want to look a little different from others.
  - I like what I see when I look in the mirror.
  - I would like to spend a year in London or Paris.
  - I like ballet.
  - I like to serve unusual dinners.
  - I really do believe that blondes have more fun.

  And disagree more than average with these statements:
  - I enjoy most forms of housework.
  - I furnish my home for comfort, not for style.
  - If it was good enough for my mother, it's good enough for me.

Moving Forward: Your Plan of Action

Business warfare is a battle for the minds of your customers, so you'll need very sophisticated weapons. Your competitors are already using the three Ps of marketing warfare: personality, positioning, and psychographics. Can you afford to do less? And they've been using them for quite some time. If you haven't, you've got a lot of catching up to do. So re-read this chapter — it's the first step in catching up with your competitors. Get other executives at your company to read it. Talk about the main ideas you got from this chapter. Eventually, put them to use. Do this, and you'll be a winning Business Warrior.

Out-Thinking
Your Competitors
THE CREATIVE BUSINESS WARRIOR

Part of the mythology of business is that nobody ever went broke underestimating the intelligence of the consumer. I disagree, big-time! Your customers are smart. And your competitors are smarter than your customers, so never underestimate them either! Your enemies are continually thinking of new ways to outmaneuver you, and you should be doing the same thing, or your share of the pie is certain to shrink. You need to become better at coming up with new and better ideas, because in today's extremely competitive marketplace you have to run faster and faster just to stay in place. This chapter will help you to out-think your enemy — and win big!

The Just-Noticeable Difference

You probably go to work the same way every morning. Think about which billboards you saw this morning on your way to work. I'll bet you can't think of any, even though you've passed by them hundreds of times. Why? Because they're *too familiar!* They've blended into the background. The only time you probably notice them is when the billboard is changed. Why?

Because of Weber's Law. You may have learned about it in your psychology classes. It says people usually don't notice relatively small differences between brands or between changes in brand attributes. The minimum amount one brand or brand attribute can differ from another with the difference noticed by most people is called the JND, or Just-Noticeable Difference. The challenge to marketers, then, is in figuring out how much change is needed for most people to notice a difference. And the greater the intensity (or level of importance to customers) of the original brand or brand attribute, the more you'll have to change the new brand or brand attribute before your customers will notice the change. Here's the math:

> The change in intensity of the attribute needed for a difference to be perceived divided by the intensity of the original attribute equals a JND constant. That constant is different for each of your five senses — sight, hearing, smell, taste, and touch. Scientists have established benchmark values for each sense. Here are two examples:

> - The JND constant for visual brightness (sight) is 0.016. (At 1,000 photons)
> - The JND constant for loudness (hearing) is 0.0909. (At 100 decibels, 1,000 cycles per second)

Marketers use the JND concept to predict customer reactions to changes in price, quality, and other brand attributes. How can you use these numbers? Well, if you *don't* want changes in your brand to be noticed, your changes should be *below* the JND. Candy bar marketers have followed this principle for years by making slight reductions in the weight of their bars instead of raising their prices.

If you *do* want your changes to be noticed, they must be *above* the JND. That's why you see the words *New and Improved* on liquid detergent labels so much. Of course, if your customers don't notice the differences, they'll think you've lied to them, and your sales will probably go down.

You may be thinking, "So What! This is interesting, but what does this have to do with getting new ideas?" Here's my answer:

It's easy to get into a rut. If you see the same billboard over and over again, you no longer notice it. It takes a big change to get you to notice it's there. And if you use the same thought processes over and over again, you'll get stuck for new ideas. If you follow the trend and do what your competitors are already doing, you'll never occupy the being-first position, which you learned was so important in Chapter 4, and your brand will be thought of as just another boring, unexciting *me-too* brand. People who make the most money in the stock market don't follow the trends. They think for themselves. They see where everybody else is going, weigh the facts, and start a new trend somewhere else. They are leaders, not followers. Do you lead, or do you follow?

Most advertising people are followers. Why? Because they're very trend-conscious. They jump on the bandwagon whenever a hot new trend occurs. They don't realize that when the pendulum has swung too far one way, the only ads customers will notice will be those that are different.

A *Beetle Bailey* cartoon put it best: General Halftrack came into the Officer's Club after work and was greeted by the bartender, who said, "The usual, General?" Halftrack replied, "No … surprise me. The usual is becoming too usual."

How Creative Are You?

When the usual is becoming too usual for you, when you are stuck for new ideas, what can you do? Let's see how many of these six characteristics you have:

- You have a high tolerance for ambiguity, so you are comfortable with half-developed ideas that are worth pursuing.

- You have a feel for when the company rulebook should be ignored and are willing to stretch company policy at those times.

- When you get a new idea or when one is presented to you, you're willing to make an on-the-spot decision.

- You're a good listener, and you build on the suggestions of your subordinates, suppliers, customers, etc.

- You don't dwell on your or others' mistakes. Instead, you're future-oriented.

- You give your employees a lot of freedom to take risks, expecting that errors will be made from time to time, and you are willing to absorb the risk of being responsible for some failures in the process.

Those are characteristics of creative *managers*. How many of those charactersitics describe you? Here are 20 characteristics of a creative *person* in general:

- Impulsive. Doesn't repress or suppress emotions, actions. Takes risks first, asks questions later.

- Enjoys and is able to communicate well with others.

- Deliberately creates conflict to create sparks that contain ideas, not to increase bad feelings between people. Loves to straighten out messes, to get involved in conflicts, and to make conflicts productive.

- Power-oriented, dominant. High level of drive and ambition.

- High confidence level, ambition, determination. Sense of destiny. Resolute.

- Prefers complexity of thought, simplicity in products.

- Unconventional thought processes. Really enjoys thinking and analyzing. Less interested in small details, more interested in overall meanings and implications.

- Ability to redefine — likes to shift ideas, concepts, objects, and people in order to use them in new ways.

- Ability to abstract, to break down complex or hard problems into smaller, more easily handled parts, and yet recognize and keep track of interrelationships.

- Ability to synthesize, to pull together seemingly unrelated ideas.

- Tolerance for ambiguity. Tolerates and even welcomes tension created by strong opposing values. Releases tension through exercise.

- Relaxed, yet attentive.

- Open-minded. Much more flexible than most people.

- Inquiring mind, skeptical. Very curious. Open to new experiences.

- Detached from tasks in which he is intellectually involved.

- More intellectual. Higher verbal fluency. Above average in intelligence.

- Has command of a wide range of information.

- Very independent judgment. Not much concerned with popularity or with "doing the right thing." Less bound by conventional moral standards, by rules and regulations. Rebellious and nonconforming.

- Hobbies and interests are quite unrelated to field of work.

- Has friends and co-workers who are also highly creative.

Again, how many of these characteristics describe you?

How Creative Is Your Organization?

Don't worry too much if you don't have too many of those 26 character-istics. You'll acquire several of them after reading this chapter. However, you probably should worry if your company stifles your creative impulse and you can do nothing to change the organization.

Maybe you should go to work for IBM. It's one of the most creative and profitable firms in the United States. Here's what IBM said in an ad:

> The story goes that Henry Ford once hired an efficiency expert to evaluate his company. After a few weeks, the expert made his report. It was highly favorable except for one thing. "It's that man down the hall," said the expert. "Every time I go by his office he's just sitting there with his feet on his desk. He's wasting your money." Ford replied, "That man once had an idea that saved us millions of dollars. At the time, I believe his feet were planted right where they are now."
>
> At IBM, we have 46 people like that, and we don't worry about where they put their feet either. They are the IBM Fellows. They earned the title by having ideas that made a difference. Their job is to have more ideas like that, but under a very special condition. It's called freedom. Freedom from deadlines. Freedom from committees. Freedom from the usual limits of corporate approval.
>
> For a term of at least five years, an IBM Fellow is free to pursue any advanced project of value to IBM, even if chances for success may seem remote. As a result, some of the great innovations of our time have come from IBM Fellows. We may not always understand what they're doing, much less how they do it. But we know this: The best way to inspire an IBM Fellow is to get out of the way.

How You Can Become *A Lot More* Creative

So how can you become more creative? There are many books and articles on this subject. Just enter the word creativity on Amazon.com and see how many titles come up. Well, maybe you don't have to buy a book on creativity. The book you're reading right now will make you a lot more creative than you are now — if you follow the suggestions I give you in this chapter. It contains highlights of a one-day seminar I've given several hundred times on the subject. Here are the seven things that work the best, according to feedback I've gotten from my audiences:

- Become more like a child.
- Brainstorm.

- Use forced relationships.
- Put judgment on hold.
- Use a bug list.
- Think of 101 uses for ….
- Find creativity-stimulating exercises and do them.

Become More Like a Child

Watch and learn from children. They are naturally creative. Over the years we've lost the creative spirit we were born with and that young children show naturally. The willingness to take risks is important, and this is where young children and adults are very different. If your risk profile is that of a chicken (see Chapter 3), you probably aren't very creative because you can't tolerate failures. Infants learn from trial and error, and failures don't discourage them from experimenting with new things.

Infancy is the age at which all human beings learn at the fastest rate. We'll never learn as fast after infancy. By the time children reach adolescence, both peer pressure from their friends and punishment for failure by teachers and parents make children more cautious, less willing to experiment, and less creative.

By the time they become executives they may be so inhibited they'll never again try something new. And this greatly inhibits our natural creativity, which we've had since infancy and still carry around inside us.

Brainstorm

Everybody's heard of brainstorming, but very few people do it correctly. The technique was developed by a famous advertising executive in 1939 as a way to creatively solve problems. Its sole purpose is to produce, in a group session, as many ideas as possible. Even poor ones — the more, the better. Here are Alex Osborn's original four rules:

- No criticism of ideas until the end of the session.
- The wilder the idea, the better.
- Quantity is wanted, not quality: The more ideas produced, the greater likelihood of useful ideas.
- Combine and improve ideas heard from others in the group to form brand-new ideas. A snowball or ricochet effect happens this way.

I've found that brainstorming to creatively solve problems works best when these additional seven suggestions are followed:

- Have six to ten people in your group. Six or seven people are best.

- The problem should be as specific as possible, and the group should be told what the problem is two days in advance of the brainstorming session so their ideas can incubate. However, don't let them talk to one another about the problem before the session itself.

- Don't have too many experts in your group, because experts have stereotyped and preset ways of looking at problems. Furthermore, if the group members know there's an expert present, they will be in awe. They'll let the expert do most of the talking, which is bad for generating ideas.

- There should be only one problem under consideration per session.

- Brainstorm for a half hour at most, because the brain gets tired after that.

- Hold the session in the morning — mornings are best; late afternoons are worst.

- Videotape the session so that you can review comments at a later time.

Use Forced Relationships

Cartoonists, who need 365 gags yearly for their newspaper comic strips, stimulate their production of ideas this way: They list many ideas on a sheet of paper. After they have a very long list, they consider each idea in relation to every other idea. Some of the combinations are ridiculous, which makes for a good newspaper cartoon gag. When you try it, some of your combinations won't make any sense, but you'll get a few gems that would have otherwise escaped you.

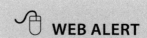

WEB ALERT

You'll find several examples of how electronics manufacturers have made big money using forced relationships at GuerrillaDon.com.

Put Judgment On Hold

In other words, don't jump to conclusions. This works if you and others around you can get rid of the negative-thinking habit. Some people who are on ego trips may shoot down new ideas just to score debating points. Try not to have those people around you. They stifle creativity.

On the other hand, you might get good results if you actively try to involve them. Try the PIN technique. PIN stands for positive, interesting, and negative. Make it a rule that whoever comments on an idea must first offer a positive comment on it, then pick out something interesting about it, and only then, if they still want to, something negative.

Use a Bug List

Name as many unsolved problems as you can, in terms of things that "bug" or disturb you. Use the list to develop starter material for producing ideas in a brainstorming session.

Think of 101 Uses For …

Think about some common object, such as a coat hanger, socks, a key, and so on, and pretend it has no known function or name. Then, name as many possible uses as you can for the item, at least 101, if possible.

Find Creativity-Stimulating Exercises and Work on Them

Many books contain fun exercises you can work on that can help you become more creative (like Sudoku). Look them up on Amazon.com. Figure 5.1 shows three examples my seminar participants especially enjoy.

1. Nine Dots: Draw four straight lines that pass through all nine dots without picking up your pencil and without retracing.

2. Six Glasses: By handling and moving only one empty glass, change the arrangement so that no empty glass is next to another empty glass, and no full glass is next to another full glass.

3. Bonus: Rearrange the letters in the nonsense word PILNEC to make it into a meaningful word.

You can find the answers in Figure 5.2. Don't peek until you solve these three problems.

NINE DOTS: Draw four straight lines that pass through all nine dots without picking up your pencil and without retracing.

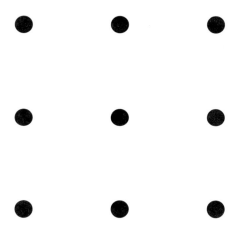

SIX GLASSES: By handling and moving only one glass, change the arrangement of glasses so that no empty glass is next to another empty glass, and no full glass is next to another full glass.

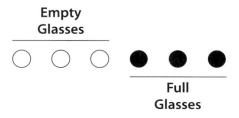

BONUS: Rearange the letters in this nonsense word to make it into a meaningful word — PILNEC.

Figure 5.1. Creativity exercise: nine dots, six glasses

NINE DOTS ANSWER: If you had problems solving this one, you probably organized the problem in your mind in terms of a very familiar pattern — a square — because that's what the nine dots look like. If you tried square and other right-angle line structures, you soon ran out of options. Eskimo children, probably because their world includes relatively few rectangular forms, solve this problem rather quickly.

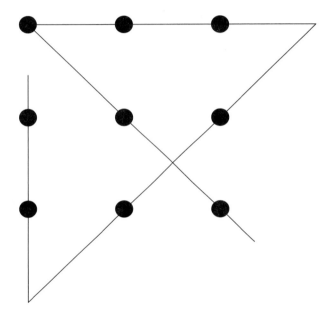

SIX GLASSES ANSWER: By picking up the middle full glass, pouring the water from it into the empty glass, and putting it back in its original position, you'll have this pattern: Empty, Full, Empty, Full, Empty, Full.

BONUS ANSWER: PILNEC = PENCIL. Pilnec looks like a plausible word because it's pronounceable and seems phonetically reasonable. Your brain clings to it at first because it forms an "acceptable" pattern in your brain. But when you begin to rearrange the letters, you break down the tyranny of the original pattern, and your brain becomes free to search for other combinations that are more acceptable.

Figure 5.2. Creativity exercise answers

Moving Forward: Your Plan of Action

Creativity is a skill, and it will take years of practicing before you become unconsciously skillful at it. When you become that skillful, you'll finally be truly creative and able to out-think your enemy. But if you don't use your creativity often enough, that very important skill will waste away, and you'll be at the mercy of your enemies in the business war you are waging. For you older readers who think "If it ain't broke, don't fix it," here's an added bonus — creative thinking, done regularly, is supposed to help prevent Alzheimer's disease.

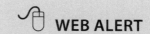 **WEB ALERT**

You'll find more suggestions on how to become more creative at GuerrillaDon. com, including Attribute Listing, Lateral Thinking, and Structural Analysis.

I'm pretty sure you enjoyed this chapter. Becoming more creative is a lot of fun. And it isn't difficult at all. But you need to practice this skill continually.

So don't despair. Creativity can be learned. If you're like most people, you were much more creative as a child than you are now, and you can be that way again. Remember what Lewis Carroll said in *Alice's Adventures in Wonderland* and *Through the Looking-Glass:*

> Alice laughed. "There's no use trying," she said. "One can't believe impossible things."
> "I daresay you haven't had much practice," said the Queen. "When I was your age, I always did it for half-an-hour a day. Why, sometimes, I've believed as many as six impossible things before breakfast."

You'll need to be like the Queen to stay ahead of your competitors.

6

The Four Battlegrounds of Business
ALL ABOUT STRATEGY

This chapter focuses on strategy, and Chapter 7 focuses on tactics. Remember that strategy is doing the right things — deciding what you should do. And tactics is all about doing things right — deciding *how* to do them. This chapter gives you a very powerful tool you need to pick the best strategy. I call this tool *The Four Battlegrounds of Business*. It's based on two very well-known strategic planning tools that you probably learned about in your first marketing course:

- Product Portfolio Analysis — from The Boston Consulting Group
- The Strategic Planning Matrix — from General Electric and McKinsey & Company.

Many companies use both grids in their strategic planning. They first classify their different strategic business units using the BCG approach and then go into greater detail with the GE method. Let's look at both these tools briefly, and then get into what I recommend — the Four Battlegrounds of Business, a combination of the best of both BCG and GE/McKinsey.

Product Portfolio Analysis — from The Boston Consulting Group

Product portfolio analysis has been around since the 1960s. Today some consultants criticize it as being overly simplistic. Maybe so, but it's also convenient and easy to remember, especially when you're just starting out in business. The basic approach is to put circles of different sizes on the grid shown in Figure 6.1.

The seven circles represent seven different brands in your company. Some circles are large, some are small. The relative sizes tell you the proportional importance of each brand's contribution to dollar volume in your company.

Relative market share (dominance) is on the horizontal axis. Take into account only your product's market share relative to its largest competitor — not to any other competitors. A relative market share of 0.2 means your product's sales volume is only 20 percent of the sales volume of the market leader. If you have a 5.0 relative market share, it means you, the market leader, have five times as much market share as your largest competitor. The dividing line is 1.0. Four brands have a relatively high share on the left side of the grid, and three brands have a relatively low share on the right side.

Market growth rate is on the vertical axis. It's the annual growth rate of the market. High growth rate is above nine percent a year. Low growth rate is below nine percent a year. Figure 6.1 tells you that the growth rate ranges between 0 percent and 18 percent a year.

- *Top left square:* High growth, big market share. Stars live here. Stars are the market leaders in a high-growth market. They require more cash than they generate. It takes a lot of money to keep Stars in orbit.

- *Top right square:* Question Marks (Problem Children) live here. These kinds of brands have a relatively low market share in a high-growth market. Like Stars, they require more cash than they generate, but usually much less than Stars.

- *Bottom left square:* Cash Cows live here. Cash Cows are the market leaders in a low-growth market. They generate more cash than they need.

- *Bottom right square:* Dogs and Losers live here. Most products are dogs. They have weak market shares in low-growth markets. Get rid of your Losers, but keep your Dogs. Don't confuse the two.

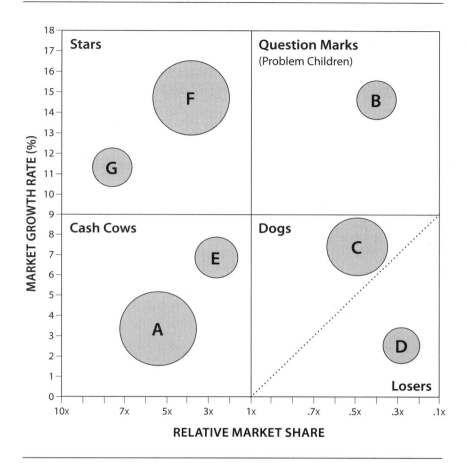

Figure 6.1. Boston Consulting Group's Growth-Share Matrix

You, the Business Warrior, have to decide how much money to invest in each brand on the matrix. Here are five questions you need to answer:

Question: Should you spend a lot of money on Dogs?

Answer: If you do this, you're really trying to gain market share against entrenched competitors. That can be disastrous! Remember what you learned back in Chapter 4 when I gave you the ins and outs of positioning.

Question: Should you get rid of your Dogs instead?

Answer: I'll answer this on the next page. But first…

Question: Is it good or bad to balance your portfolio?

Answer: It's not only good, it's very, very good. Don't have *too many* Question Marks (Problem Children), Dogs, and Losers. Don't have too few Stars and Cash Cows.

Question: How do you balance your portfolio?

Answer:

- *Build.* Increase your brand's market share, even if you have to give up short-term earnings to get that market share. This is appropriate for Question Marks (Problem Children) that you want to become Stars.

- *Hold.* Instead of increasing your brand's market share, you want only to preserve it. This is appropriate for strong Cash Cows. You want to keep that big cash flow coming.

- *Harvest.* Increase your product's short-term cash flow, even at the expense of its long-term cash flow prospects. This is appropriate for weak Cash Cows, as well as for Dogs and Question Marks (Problem Children).

- *Divest.* Sell or liquidate the brand so that you can use your resources better somewhere else. Do this for Question Marks (Problem Children) that are drags on your profits. However, don't be too quick to want to get rid of your Dogs, because most products *are* Dogs. Notice the dotted line in the bottom right of the grid in Figure 6.1. If your Dog is on the right side of the dotted line, it's probably wise to get rid of it. Why? Because that brand *isn't* a Dog, it's a Loser. If your Dog is on the left side, it really *is* a Dog, and you should keep it around for a while. After all, Dogs are lovable creatures and are quite useful to many companies. Feed them gourmet dog food, pet and pamper them, and they may even turn into Cash Cows.

Question: Why is product portfolio analysis a good tool for planning your marketing strategy?

Answer: Most products start off as Question Marks (Problem Children), move into the Star category, then into Cash Cows if things go well, and finally into Dogs toward the end of their product life cycle. Therefore, you need to concentrate not just on the current positions of your products on the matrix, but on where they will be in the future — their desired and actual future positions.

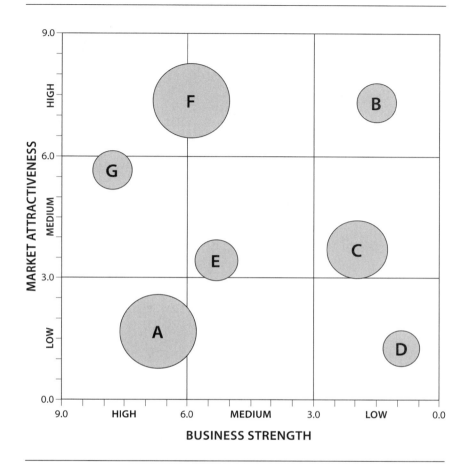

Figure 6.2. GE/McKinsey's Strategic Planning Matrix

Analyze your product's changing positions over a several-year period as part of your strategic plan, beginning a few years in the past and projecting its trajectory over the matrix several years into the future. If its projected trajectory looks bad, then you should come up with a new strategy to change the trajectory, or come up with new products.

The Strategic Planning Matrix—from General Electric and McKinsey & Company

Figure 6.2 shows the equally popular strategic planning tool that was pioneered by the General Electric Company, working with McKinsey &

Company, a leading management consulting firm. You can see the three main differences:

- GE/McKinsey calls the horizontal axis *Business Strength* instead of *Relative Market Share*. And it calls the vertical axis *Market Attractiveness* instead of *Market Growth Rate*.

- GE/McKinsey is more complicated because it uses a nine-cell grid instead of a four-cell grid.

- GE/McKinsey quantifies Business Strength and Market Attractiveness better than BCG quantifies Relative Market Share and Market Growth Rate.

The Four Battlegrounds of Business Matrix — from Guerrilla Don Hendon

Here's my contribution. I've combined the best features of the BCG and GE/McKinsey matrices and have eliminated their minor weaknesses. For example, I don't like the words Star and Dog. Emotionally, our egos want us to become Stars (even though we know it costs too much money to keep a Star in orbit), and nobody wants to end up with a brand that's a Dog. Also, in some industries, a 10 percent market growth rate would be very high, but in others, a 20 percent market growth rate would be extremely low. On the other hand, it's easier to plan using a four-cell matrix instead of a nine-cell matrix. The *stark naked* version of my Four Battlegrounds of Business Matrix is shown in Figure 6.3. (The *fully clothed* version is Figure 7.2. Check it out now if you want. It's on page 110.)

My matrix uses the simpler four cells of the BCG matrix and the more appealing nomenclature of the GE/McKinsey matrix. I made sure The Four Battlegrounds of Business Matrix mirrors both:

- The underlying logic of the matrix is easy to understand.

- It's easy to get the data needed to analyze your product portfolios.

- The matrix uses simple terms — the horizontal axis is *Attraction* and the vertical axis is *Strength*.

- Both axes use a scale from 1 to 5.

Let's look at the situations you'll encounter as well as strategies you might employ in each of the four battlegrounds. But first, where does

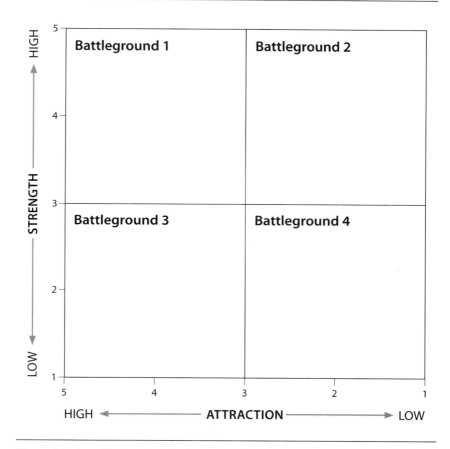

Figure 6.3. Guerrilla Don Hendon's Four Battlegrounds of Business Matrix — *stark naked* version

your brand lie in the Four Battlegrounds of Business Matrix? With Figure 6.3 in front of you, get your brand group together and ask them to do three things:

- Come up with a bunch of attraction and strength factors.

- Assign weights to them. Weights should add up to 1.00.

- Rate each factor, using a whole number between 1 and 5, reflecting how your brand stands on that factor.

ATTRACTION Factors	Weight adds up to 1.00	Rating 1 to 5	Final value weight x rating
Overall market size	0.20	4	0.80
Annual market growth rate	0.20	5	1.00
Historical profit margin	0.15	4	0.60
Competitive intensity	0.15	2	0.30
Technological requirements	0.15	3	0.45
Vulnerability to inflation	0.05	3	0.15
Energy requirements	0.05	2	0.10
Environmental impact	0.05	1	0.05
Social-political-legal	Must be acceptable	Must be acceptable	Must be acceptable
Total	1.00		3.45

Figure 6.4. Placing your brand on the Four Battlegrounds of Business Matrix — Attraction

Confused? Probably. End your confusion by looking at this example. It shows you how to do it, using nine factors for Attraction and twelve factors for Strength.

In this example (Figure 6.4), I gave the brand — call it Brand Alpha — a 4 on overall market size, indicating it is pretty high — a 5 would be *extremely* high. And I gave it a weight of 0.20. You have to multiply the weights by the ratings to arrive at the values, so overall market size has a final value of 0.80. I did the same for the remaining factors and came up with a final value of 3.45. That's the brand's Attraction score.

STRENGTH Factors	Weight adds up to 1.00	Rating 1 to 5	Final value weight x rating
Market share	0.10	4	0.40
Share growth	0.15	4	0.60
Product quality	0.10	4	0.40
Brand reputation	0.10	5	0.50
Distribution network	0.05	4	0.20
Effectiveness of promotion	0.05	5	0.25
Production capacity	0.05	3	0.15
Production efficiency	0.05	2	0.10
Unit costs	0.15	3	0.45
Material supplies	0.05	5	0.25
Research and development performance	0.10	4	0.40
Quality of managers	0.05	4	0.20
Total	1.00		3.90

Figure 6.5. Placing your brand on the Four Battlegrounds of Business Matrix — Strength

Now look at Alpha's Strength (Figure 6.5). I followed the same procedure for each of the 12 factors and came up with a final value of 3.90. In my example, Alpha scored a 3.45 on Attraction and a 3.90 on Strength, out of a possible maximum score of 5 for each.

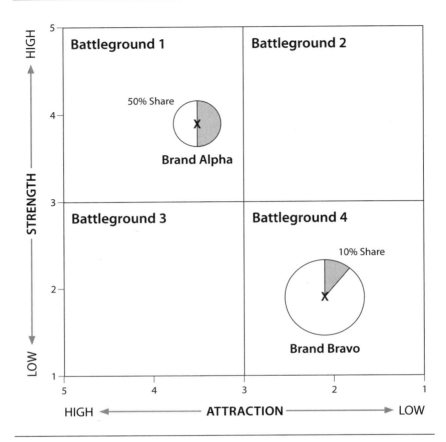

**Figure 6.6. Guerrilla Don Hendon's Four Battlegrounds of Business Matrix —
with circles**

What do you do next? Look at Battleground 1 in Figure 6.6. Here's
what I did there:

- I put an X at the intersection of 3.45 (Attraction) and 3.90
  (Strength). And I drew a circle around it. The shaded area
  indicates Alpha's market share. It's a dominant brand in its
  category and enjoys a 50 percent share. However, Alpha only
  brings a small amount of revenue to your company. So the
  circle is small. The category is growing rapidly, so it's in a very
  attractive market.

- Your company also markets another product. Call it Brand Bravo. Let's say you did the same analysis and came up with 2.1 (Attraction) and 1.9 (Strength). I put the X at that intersection. Bravo is in Battleground 4. Its market share is only 10 percent, but it brings in three times more revenue to your company than Alpha does. So Bravo's circle is three times larger than Alpha's circle. However, the market that Bravo is in isn't growing — overall sales for all companies have been declining steadily for the last five years.

You're the marketing manager for both these brands. What are you going to do? Will you milk Bravo for as long as you can, enjoy its revenue, and let it die a natural death? Will you take Bravo's cash flow and spend it on Alpha and try to increase its market share even more than 50 percent? Or will you try your luck by coming up with a third brand in a completely different product category?

Good questions, but they're hypothetical. Let's get real. It's time for you to do what I did, but this time with *your* brands and data. And remember the old GIGO rule — garbage in, garbage out. Make sure you're not just making up figures and blowing smoke. What's next?

Here's where your planning comes in. Remember how much we talked about it in Chapter 3? That's the second longest chapter in this book — around 7,500 words! If you don't think you know how to plan, re-read Chapter 3 right now. It begins on page 35.

If you think you can plan for the future pretty well, then here's what to do next:

First, do the same analysis for all the brands you're responsible for. Put them in one of my four Battlegrounds of Business. Show the market shares. Make the sizes of the circles proportional to their revenue flow.

Second, plot the projected positions of each of your brands on the Battlegrounds matrix, where you expect/want your brands to be 12 months from now. Draw the new circles with dotted lines to differentiate them.

Third, here's the most important thing to do: Determine what strategies and tactics are needed to move your brands to their desired positions in the Battlegrounds matrix. This is where you, Business Warrior, earn your salary and bonus and get your promotion. The next four parts of this chapter and all of Chapter 7 will help you in moving your brands to the positions you want. Chapter 7 begins on page 107.

Business Battleground 1: High Attraction, High Strength — Similar to BCG's Star

The Situation

- This is a market with a lot of present and potential attraction for you and your enemies. (Let's start calling your competitors enemies now. After all, you're in a war with them!)
- Your business army holds a dominant or significant share of the total business. You are *king of the mountain*. This is a profitable cell to be in.
- It's exciting to your ego to be involved with a brand in this cell — not much to worry about.

Strategic Principles of Business Warfare

- Stay dominant at all costs.
- Counterattack *any* upstart.
- Pursue and smash any significant enemy ruthlessly as a warning to new enemies who may be attracted to this market.
- Don't give up control of the situation. Stay on the attack, maintaining your momentum.
- Don't be predictable. Keep your enemy off-balance.

Business Battleground 2: Low Attraction, High Strength — Similar to BCG's Cash Cow

The Situation

- This market is already heavily penetrated by you and your enemies, with very little room for growth or profits.
- Your business army is still king of the mountain, with a dominant or a significant share of the total business.
- You worry more here than you would in Business Battleground 1.

- There's an exception — a niche market: This is a small market that's unattractive to big companies because of its small size. But it's a market that can be very profitable for an entrepreneur who wants to concentrate efforts there.

Strategic Principles of Business Warfare

- Make your enemies think your position is stronger than it is by keeping in control of the situation, not abandoning your leadership, staying on the attack, and keeping your momentum. Maintain an aura of vicious invulnerability.

- Use the BCG's hold strategy and preserve your market share.

- Keep a lot of money in reserve so that you can counterattack as viciously as possible with a mobile strike force.

- Increase profitability not by drastic economizing but by cutting costs selectively if necessary. Drastic economizing will weaken you.

- Seek opportunities to demoralize your enemies whenever possible. After all, you've got the cash flow to do it.

Business Battleground 3: High Attraction, Low Strength — Similar to BCG's Question Marks (Problem Children)

The Situation

- Again, you're in a market with much present and potential attraction for your enemies and you.

- You'll take falcon-size risks to win here because your business army holds only a subordinate position. (Remember the falcon? If not, go back to Chapter 3, pages 55 – 56.)

- You worry even more here than you would in Battleground 2.

Strategic Principles of Business Warfare

- Make a realistic assessment of your chances of winning, or you'll find yourself in too many of these battlegrounds.

- If you feel that you have a realistically good chance of winning, concentrate your forces and attack the enemy on a narrow front. Use the BCG's build strategy and increase your market share.

- If you're not prepared for the risk, either cut costs selectively or tend to your wounds, cut your losses, get out, and enter new battlegrounds at a later date. Don't economize drastically or you'll be bled to death by your enemy.

- Use the BCG's harvest strategy (increase your brand's short-term cash flow) or divest strategy (sell or liquidate your brand) here.

Business Battleground 4: Low Attraction, Low Strength — Similar to BCG's Dog

The Situation

- Once more, you're in a market that is already heavily penetrated by both you and your enemies, with very little room for growth (and profitability).

- The falcon-size risks you'd take in Battleground 3 aren't as big here because your enemies probably won't be too interested in a low-attraction market.

- Your only worry is to make the right choice — stay in or get out. It's hard to get rid of a loser, though. Here's why:

  - It may be part of your company's tradition.

  - You've already put so much time and money into it. (Note: This is a dumb mistake. See Preparation Weapon 13 in Chapter 11, page 184.)

  - It's usually easier to keep the status quo than to go through all the trouble of getting rid of it.

  - Some top executives may be associated with the brand.

But remember what Sun Tzu said: No king should put soldiers into combat merely to satisfy his ego …. No general should fight a battle simply out of resentment and spite.

Strategic Principles of Business Warfare

- Retreating armies used to burn the crops behind them, but you shouldn't use this *scorched earth* policy. Why waste time, effort, and money in a lost cause?

- A contested withdrawal is better for your ego and your troops' morale than is an all-out rout. So even if you're an old bull put out to pasture, make noises like a young and virile bull so the new bull won't think you're another cow to ravage.

Moving Forward: Your Plan of Action

Generally speaking, here's what you see in most markets:

- One leader in Business Battleground 1. The leader plays defense most of the time.

- Two strong number twos in Business Battleground 2. They often use the frontal attack.

- Three medium-size companies in Battleground 3. They usually use the flanking or wing attacks.

- Ninety-four also-rans in Battleground 4. They should use guerrilla warfare.

You're probably saying to yourself right now, "Hey, wait a minute! Don Hendon hasn't talked about defense, frontal attacks, flanking attacks, wing attacks, and guerrilla attacks yet. Why is this here?"

You're right — these are all tactics — how to do things right, as opposed to picking what things to do — the right things, of course (strategy). What I just said is a preview of what you'll learn in Chapter 7; you'll be there pretty soon. Right now there are just a few more things you need to know before you can move forward.

First, you shouldn't think that just because you happen to be in Battleground 1, you should use only defensive tactics. You're really in more than one battleground, when you think about it. Most of you live and work in the United States, a very big nation. And you don't enjoy the same strength in each geographic or demographic market. Each of these markets is different in terms of attraction as well.

And so, I say be flexible — you've got to use different tactics at the same time in different areas. Generals who win wars always use a combination of tactics in their battlegrounds. And so should business executives. If you're on defense in one market (Battleground 1), you can still be on the frontal attack in a second market (Battleground 2), on a wing or flank attack in a third market (Battleground 3), and a guerrilla attack in a fourth market (Battleground 4) — all with the same brand. After all, there are a lot of different markets out there.

Now let's move on to Chapter 7, where you'll learn not only what tactics to use in which Business Battleground but what tactics to use at each stage of the product life cycle.

Offensive and Defensive Weapons
ALL ABOUT TACTICS

You're going to learn *how* to do the right things in this chapter. You've left the realm of strategy (selecting the right things to do). You've entered the wonderful world of tactics. Because tactics are harder to master than strategy, this chapter has to be more detailed than Chapter 6. Many more specific suggestions are given here. You'll learn what tactics to use in each Business Battleground. You'll also learn what tactics to use in each stage of your product's life cycle. You'll have 70 of them to choose from here.

Strategic and Tactical Attacks

Let's begin by defining the four tactical attack formations — and one more kind of strategy, the enveloping attack. Look at Figure 7.1.

The *enveloping attack* is a move into major new market areas. By doing so, the Business Warrior changes the way the business is done. For example, camcorders have wiped out the home-movie business as it traditionally operated, using motion-picture film cameras. This created opportunities for flexible Business Warriors and disaster for shortsighted executives. Enveloping moves are strategic in nature. The rest of Chapter 7 is all about tactics.

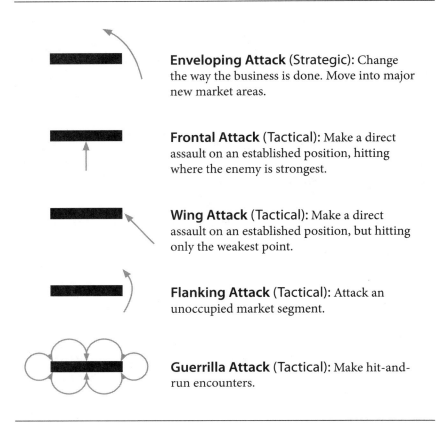

Enveloping Attack (Strategic): Change the way the business is done. Move into major new market areas.

Frontal Attack (Tactical): Make a direct assault on an established position, hitting where the enemy is strongest.

Wing Attack (Tactical): Make a direct assault on an established position, but hitting only the weakest point.

Flanking Attack (Tactical): Attack an unoccupied market segment.

Guerrilla Attack (Tactical): Make hit-and-run encounters.

Figure 7.1. Strategic and tactical attack formations

The *frontal attack* is a direct assault on an established enemy position. It's the riskiest kind of warfare. My advice:

- Avoid it unless your numerical superiority is overwhelming and you can afford to spend *a lot* of money.
- Keep in mind the lesson of the Square Army versus the Star Army (Figures 4.1 to 4.4, pages 69 – 72), and have at least a three-to-one advantage.
- Don't be overconfident and take falcon-size risks without evaluating the situation thoroughly.
- Choose your target wisely. Ask yourself if you can afford heavy costs and casualties. If you can't, don't do it.

- It's appropriate for the extremely strong companies in Business Battlegrounds 1 and 2, but not for the weaker companies in Business Battlegrounds 3 and 4. Chapter 9, "Winning Business Warfare the Big Dog's Way," gives you many more details about the principles of business warfare for a frontal attack.

The *wing attack* is a modified frontal attack. Here you're hitting only the weak point of an enemy's position. You're going after a segment they are weak in.

The *flanking attack* is similar to a wing attack. Here you're attacking an unoccupied market segment by making an *end run* around your enemy's position in the marketplace. Since the segment is unoccupied, your attack will probably go uncontested.

Wing and flanking attacks are most appropriate for weaker companies, especially for those in Battleground 3.

Finally, the *guerrilla attack* is a hit-and-run type of attack. Guerrillas need to find a market small enough to defend and big enough to live on. This attack is the most flexible of all. Chapter 8, "Winning Business Warfare the Guerrilla Way," gives you the principles of guerrilla warfare you'll need to win your guerrilla battles.

Winning Tactics to Use in the Four Battlegrounds of Business

Look at Figure 7.2. Does it look familiar? It should. It's my Four Battlegrounds of Business Matrix (Stark Naked Version), and you saw it in Chapter 6. Go back there and look at Figure 6.3. It's on page 97. Instead of nothing in the four squares back in Chapter 6, the matrix is now fully clothed. Here in Chapter 7 you see what tactics to use in each of the four battlegrounds. And other important stuff.

Here are seven important things to know about Figure 7.2.

First. In most markets, the top two brands are usually either in Battlegrounds 1 or 2, the third-place brand is usually in Battleground 3, and the fourth-place brand is usually in Battleground 4. All the other also-rans are also in Battleground 4.

Second. The two most appropriate tactics to use in Battlegrounds 1 and 2 are the frontal attack if you're the market leader — or defense if you're not.

Third. Wing or flanking attacks are appropriate for Battleground 3; guerrilla attacks or abandoning the market is appropriate for Battleground 4.

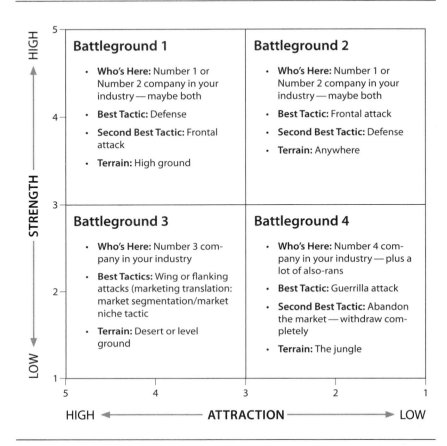

Figure 7.2. Guerrilla Don Hendon's Four Battlegrounds of Business Matrix — *fully clothed* version

You'll notice I said abandoning the market, not retreat. Why? Because this is a book about aggressive marketing, not passive marketing. Retreat, hell!

On the other hand, when you're in the decline stage of your product life cycle, you should retreat for a while. Regroup, come up with new ideas, and then attack again in the rejuvenation stage of your product life cycle. You'll learn about this later on in this chapter, pages 112 – 115.

Fourth. In Battleground 1, if you're not the leader, you're always on the defense because a lot of competitors are always showing up to take some of this attractive market away from you. Defense is a little less flexible than a frontal attack, and a lot less flexible than a guerrilla attack. And it requires a very large amount of resources.

The words *Retreat, hell!* are part of two famous sayings, both by the U.S. Marines. In World War I, Captain Lloyd Williams told a French officer who ordered a general retreat, "Retreat, hell! We just got here!" In the Korean War, General Oliver Smith said, "Retreat, hell! We're just advancing in a different direction!" You just gotta love those Marines!

Fifth. In Battleground 2, if you're not the market leader, you've got to be on the offensive, big-time! So go all-out: Use the frontal attack. It can be done on any kind of terrain, in any kind of market. It has a more likely chance of success, of course, if you frontally attack a much weaker competitor, but not if you cross over into Battleground 1 to do battle with the leading marketer. Being on offense is a lot more flexible than being on defense. However, it requires extensive resources to be successful, especially because frontal attacks are the riskiest forms of warfare. When you read about the Square Army vs. the Star Army (see Figures 4.1 to 4.4, pages 69 – 72), you realized that you would lose a lot of your resources in frontal attacks. And, if your enemy is strongly entrenched, you'll probably lose. The rest of this chapter discusses the various kinds of attacks. And many kinds of defenses, too.

Sixth. In Battleground 3, where the resources you require are rather low, attacking a market segment or market niche (using a wing or flanking attack) is best. Although this is less flexible than a guerrilla attack, it has a high probability of success if you do a good job in picking the right market segment to attack. In military battles, wing or flanking attacks are more successful where troops have no problem maneuvering, such as in a desert or on any level ground with no natural obstacles to overcome. In marketing terms, if your competitor places obstacles in your path such as hot deals to the trade whenever you try a wing or flanking attack against them, then you'll find it harder to succeed.

Seventh. In Battleground 4, the guerrilla attack tactic is the most appropriate one in most cases. This is the most flexible tactic of all because you are attacking targets of opportunity and then retreating into the jungle underbrush. Find a target market small enough to attack and big enough to live on, and you'll succeed. You don't need much in the way of resources to be a guerrilla. You'll learn a lot more about guerrilla warfare in Chapter 8. It begins on page 131.

Winning Tactics to Use in Each Stage of Your Product's Life Cycle

Things change over time. We all get older. So do our brands. When we're adolescents, we're full of energy. We look forward to what the future brings. When we get old, we aren't as active. We're nostalgic about the past. The same thing happens to our children, our brands. We use different methods to nurture them along during their lives. The rest of Chapter 7 is about the tactics to use at each stage of your product's life cycle.

First things first. Remember you're a marketing tactician. As such, you must accept the strategic position you get from your bosses as a given. It's your constraint. If you don't agree with it, try to change your bosses' minds about the overall strategy. If you can't change their minds, then grit your teeth, work within the guidelines of that strategy, and choose your tactics accordingly. Remember what you learned in Chapter 3 — how three different strategies affect five tactical decisions. It's in Step 3 of the planning process. Look at it again now. It's on page 40.

Now turn your attention to Figure 7.3. It's my version of the product life cycle. It has six stages instead of the usual four *(introduction, growth, maturity, decline)*. The extra two are the *product development* stage that happens before you introduce your product to the market and the *rejuvenation* stage that follows the decline stage.

Product Development Stage

Here's what happens in the product development stage:

- Initial idea development
- Laboratory development
- Test market
- Pilot plant development
- Semi-commercial plant trials
- Commercial startup
- Initial production

Introduction Stage

The introduction stage begins when you bring the product to market for the first time. Sales are usually slow while demand builds among

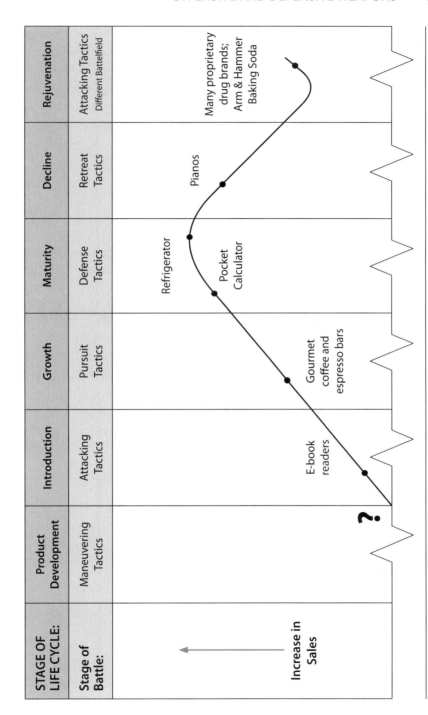

Figure 7.3. The product life cycle and six stages of battle

distributors and final consumers. You have heavy expenses here. You're overspending, and your competitors are overreacting. As a result, there are usually very little, if any, profits at this stage — even if you charge a high price for your product or service.

Growth Stage

You have rapid market acceptance in the growth stage. Profits improve sharply because your per unit production costs drop.

Maturity Stage

In the maturity stage, the rate of sales growth slows down. Most of your volume comes from repeat sales, because most buyers have already bought your product at least once by now, and few new customers are trying it. You're battling more and more competitors who entered the market during the growth and maturity stages, so prices are down and promotion costs are up. Toward the end of the maturity stage, profits may go down. However, the beginning of this stage is usually your most profitable period, so try to extend it as long as you possibly can.

Decline Stage

Sales drift downward during the decline stage as your buyers turn toward newer products entering the marketplace. Eventually your product becomes a dog and most or all profits disappear. You either give up and get out or start to think about rejuvenating your product in some way to start a brand-new life cycle.

Rejuvenation Stage

You can move your brand into the rejuvenation stage by making use of one or more of these six tactics:

- Create a major product improvement.
- Reposition the consumer's perception of your product.
- Use new distribution outlets.
- Find new uses for your product.
- Find new markets for your product.
- Develop line extensions.

Arm & Hammer Baking Soda used the rejuvenation stage very successfully when it suggested putting an open box of baking soda inside the refrigerator to eliminate bad odors. They also later advertised putting it in your swimming pool, your cat litter box, and other places. Eventually, they extended their line of products to include rug deodorizers, detergents, and other products used to clean and deodorize.

Look what Oreo cookies have evolved into: minis, double stuff, reduced fat, ice cream treats, and cookie bars. In addition to the classic white filling, there is now chocolate, mint, coffee, peanut butter and, for Halloween, orange fillings.

You can probably think of many of your competitors who have come up with new uses for old products and other tactics for extending the life of their product. Don't let them have all the fun — and profits. Think about trying it yourself. Chapter 5, "Out-Thinking Your Competitors: The Creative Business Warrior," is all about developing new product ideas. It begins on page 79.

What Stage of the Product Life Cycle Are You in?

Why should you care what stage of the product life cycle your brand is in? Because your marketing tactics change in each stage of the life cycle. So you've got to know the stage of each of your brands. Guessing wrong can be disastrous. Check out the Dow Chemical story on the next page.

The Product Life Cycle: Battle Tactics

Here are the tactics you should use at each stage of the product life cycle. I call them the Battle Tactics. Business Warriors who use them will not only win, they'll win big!

- In the product development stage, use maneuvering tactics.

- In the introduction stage, use attacking tactics.

- In the growth stage, use pursuit tactics.

- In the maturity stage, use defense tactics.

- In the decline stage, use retreat tactics. (Not abandon-the-market tactics, because you're planning to come back.)

- In the rejuvenation stage, use attacking tactics again, but in a different battlefield.

The Perils of Not Knowing the Product Life Cycle Stage of Your Brand

Dow Chemical Corporation, for example, introduced Dowtherm 209, a heavy-duty antifreeze. The company aimed it at the owners of heavy-duty diesel and gasoline trucks and other heavy-equipment owners. Instead of ethylene glycol (what most antifreeze is made of), Dowtherm 209 is a propanol product. If it leaks into the crankcase it doesn't create any problems. Ethylene glycol antifreezes cause bearing damage, cylinder scoring, and other problems if they leak into the crankcase.

Dow figured it had an important competitive advantage, so it marketed its new antifreeze as if it were a new product in the introduction stage of the life cycle. It had a very high selling price (about twice that of regular antifreeze) and heavy promotional expenditures.

However, the product's target market felt that leakage into the crankcase was not a major problem because it happened so seldom. As a result, purchasing agents thought Dowtherm was just another me-too product, in the maturity stage of the life cycle for all antifreezes. It had no important differential advantage, and it cost twice as much as regular antifreeze, so they didn't buy it.

Learn from Dow's Mistake

Make sure you know what stage of the life cycle you're in so you can pick the right marketing tactics to use. Here's a good rule of thumb: Find out what the bulk of your target customers think of your product. If they think it's brand-new, it's in the introduction stage. If they think it's just another me-too product, and if they have a poor opinion of the differential advantage you think so highly of, it's probably at the maturity or even the decline stage. Of course, the only way to find out what the bulk of your target market thinks is to do market research.

The Product Development Stage: Maneuvering Tactics

The Situation

- Prepare to learn about the marketplace and your enemy's actual and potential strengths and weaknesses.

- Try hard to discover any product weaknesses you might have so that you can correct them before launching your product.

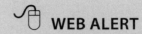 **WEB ALERT**

For three good shortcuts to finding out what your target market thinks, visit GuerrillaDon.com.

- Make a heavy investment in marketing intelligence.

- Have logistics plans ready for implementation. Send POPs (point of purchase materials) and fact sheets to sales reps. Dig deeper and find out more about the U.S. Army Quartermaster Corps, the logistical arm of the U.S. Army.

Maneuvering Tactics

- Maintain heavy security so that the enemy won't discover your intentions. Be careful about using *teaser* presale promotions. Your competitors will find out pretty quickly.

- Build up your marketing capability. Create whatever new marketing resource capabilities your brand requires. If security needs predominate, test your marketing weapons in the laboratory, not in the field (use focus groups, laboratory stores, etc.).

- Build up your service capability.

- Keep your enemies off-balance if they penetrate your curtain of secrecy. Threaten several targets until you discover their weaknesses.

- Be extremely flexible. You may have to change plans at a moment's notice.

- Develop several scenarios. Pick several sets of tactics to use in different situations. Concentrate on plans for getting distribution.

- Don't be overconfident. Remember the lesson of the square army and the star army in Chapter 4, pages 69 – 72. Add non-frontal attacks to your tactical package.

- Make extensive use of PERT (program evaluation and review technique) charts to help you keep track of what you're getting into (See Figure 7.4). Here are the basics:

  - Lay out related tasks in paths according to the order in which they'll be completed.

  - Use parallel paths for independent tasks.

  - Estimate how much time is required to complete each task and sum up the total times for each path.

  - The longest path, called the *critical path,* tells you how much time is required for the launch.

  - If you want to launch your product earlier, direct your resources to the critical path to shorten it.

  - Set up a monitoring system to track the launch.

The Introduction Stage: Attacking Tactics

The Situation

- This is your first major contact with the market and the enemy, so unveil your product as a major publicity event with heavy propaganda.

- Your objective is to penetrate deeply and quickly — establish a beachhead, as the military would say.

- Spend heavily to buy market share — but realize that there will be a high cost per market share point gain.

- Your enemies may overreact to your attack. And so there will be a loss of resources on both sides.

Attacking Tactics

- Attack your enemy with speed and surprise, always staying on the offensive.

- Establish a beachhead quickly by building primary demand. Use your heavy guns, such as heavy promotional spending, to soften up the enemy's position. You may want to charge high prices to skim the market.

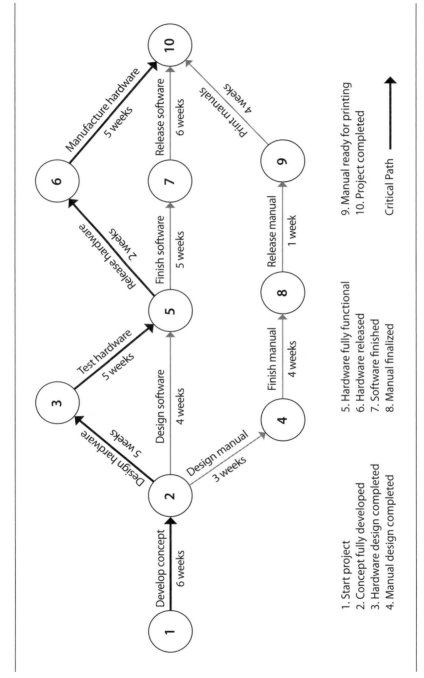

1. Start project
2. Concept fully developed
3. Hardware design completed
4. Manual design completed

5. Hardware fully functional
6. Hardware released
7. Software finished
8. Manual finalized

9. Manual ready for printing
10. Project completed

Critical Path ➝

Figure 7.4. Program evaluation and review technique (PERT) chart

- Increase the size of your beachhead by heavy use of your marketing arsenal of weapons: promoting your brand, targeting new segments, dropping unprofitable segments, improving product quality, enhancing believability of your message, using sales promotion, etc.

- Avoid a frontal attack unless you have overwhelming (at least three-to-one) numerical superiority, so choose your target wisely. The highest risk is here, so don't take falcon-size risks if you can't afford to lose. Avoid overconfidence.

- Make sure your advertising copy is effective and that you're spending sufficiently on media.

- Use your public relations agency to generate customer enthusiasm and demoralize your enemy.

- Target early adopters — both final consumers and distributors — for high awareness levels. Use them as commandos to gain brand acceptance from the total market. Get and keep distribution.

- Keep your battle plans simple (KISS them — see Chapter 3, page 61). Give buyers few, simple, and relevant reasons to purchase and repurchase.

- Coordinate all your supporting forces.

- Troubleshoot to solve all technical problems: product, shipping, service, etc.

- Avoid crash programs and hurried launches if at all possible. Try for a launch with a normal amount of pressure on all Business Warriors in your company.

- Inspire your troops (sales force and distributors) through *personal* leadership — with many trips to the field. But watch your travel expenses. You don't want to get in trouble with your bosses for lavishly overspending.

- Don't spread yourself too thin. Get overwhelming superiority by concentrating your forces on a narrow front and attack fiercely. Hit your enemy at their weakest position with combined weaponry. Figure 7.5 shows you the way the U.S. Army concentrates its forces.

It's easier to defend a position with interior lines.

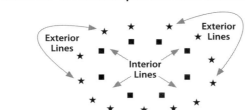

Attacking is more flexible with interior lines: Square Army attacks over a 360° range.

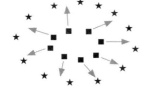

Concentrated forces lead to easier reinforcement, mutual support, and higher troop morale.

Logistical efficiency is greater when one logistics unit can support several troop units.

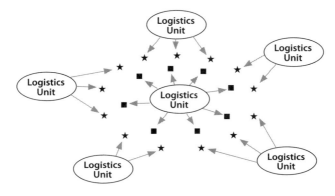

Figure 7.5. Concentrating your forces offers advantages: an example from the U.S. Army

The Army says you gain four advantages when you concentrate your resources along a narrow front:

1. *Better defense.* It's much easier to defend a position with interior lines. You have a strongly entrenched position behind a perimeter. *Marketing translation:* You own that particular territory or terrain. Attacking is also more flexible than if you have exterior lines. With exterior lines, you can only attack the enemy you've surrounded. With interior lines, you can attack in a 360-degree area. *Marketing translation:* You can expand to other markets very easily.

2. *Easier reinforcement and mutual support.* One battlefield unit is close enough to another unit to help to reinforce it when needed. *Marketing translation:* You can shift your sales reps around from one place to another much more easily and quickly if they're all close together. You do this whenever problems come up in one area or when you have a temporary work overload in a certain location.

3. *Improved troop morale.* Morale is higher when you concentrate your strength in a small area and you can get more out of your troops. It's easier to train them and to obtain new recruits. Potential soldiers have already become aware of your good reputation in the area, and you're not an outsider to them. *Marketing translation:* Sales reps who feel, think, and act like winners eventually become winners. It's a self-fulfilling prophecy.

4. *More efficient logistics.* When each troop unit requires separate support, logistical efficiency is poor. This happens with exterior lines. With interior lines, one logistics unit can support all your troop units. *Marketing translation:* All you need is one advertising campaign if you're concentrated in one area. You'd need several if your targets are dispersed.

The Growth Stage: Pursuit Tactics

The Situation

- Your objective changes here because you're growing.
- Expand your beachhead.
- Move onto the high ground so you can be king of the hill.
- The market becomes more normal than in the introduction stage. You're no longer overspending, and your enemies are no longer overreacting, so gains come at lower cost per market share point.
- You're in Battleground 1 or 3 now because the market is still growing.

Pursuit Tactics

- Maintain leadership and momentum at all costs.
- Continue your offensive attacks and broaden your beachheads.
- Go after your enemy by ruthlessly crushing all their defensive positions — if you're strong enough.
- Remember what the famous samurai warrior Miyamoto Musashi said: "When the enemy starts to collapse, you must pursue him without letting the chance go. If you fail to take advantage of your enemies' collapse, they may recover."
- Improve your weaponry. Try a penetration pricing technique, shoot for intensive distribution, try mass marketing advertising, etc.
- Gather intelligence to discover gaps in your marketplace.
- Get ideas for fresh promotional themes, market-broadening channels, and product-improvement trends.
- Keep your flanks secure to keep your enemy from surprising you with new battles.
- Pay attention to logistics. Keep the distribution pipeline filled and have heavy inventories at all levels.
- Continue to keep your enemy off-balance by being unpredictable.
- Stay very flexible by keeping a sufficient amount of money in reserve. This is your mobile strike force to exploit any opportunities you discover. Use it wisely and well.

The Maturity Stage: Defense Tactics

The Situation

- Once again your objective changes somewhat: Maintain your position as king of the hill if you're number one. It's harder to move up to number one at this stage if you're an also-ran, though.

- This is often a very profitable phase for you and your competitors, especially at the beginning, but it's somewhat less profitable at the end of the maturity stage.

- The Business Battleground may shift from 1 or 3 to 2 or 4 because market growth has slowed, demand is faltering, or competition is stronger but from fewer competitors.

- There are fewer surprises from customers and enemies. Stability is the norm now.

Defense Tactics

- Defense is the same thing as offense in that *the best defense is a good offense,* so continue to attack aggressively. The difference is that, in defense, the *defender* picks the battlefield. By the way, both General Clausewitz and famous prizefighter Jack Dempsey both said this. This saying is often used in sports.

- The battlefield should be over profits from your *enemy's* customers, not from *your* customers. Sun Tzu said that a wise general makes sure his troops feed on the enemy, for one cartload of the enemy's supplies is equal to twenty of our own.

- Never be predictable. Be flexible enough to keep your enemy off balance.

- Maintain the illusion of overwhelming strength to keep the enemy scared of you. Go after your enemy, make their life miserable. If you don't succeed, *your* life may become miserable!

- Make sure your enemy knows you're mean and nasty. Budweiser reminds everybody it's the king of beers, striking fear into the heart of Coors Beer and making Bud drinkers feel like kings themselves.

- Have the right attitude: "I've earned my position and profits, so I'll defend them fiercely." Be overprotective of the franchise you've developed.

- Counterattack any incursion to dislodge any enemy penetration.

- Have great superiority in numbers on the battlefield whenever you go to battle with the enemy. Keep remembering the lessons of the Square Army versus the Star Army. (See Chapter 4.)

- Look for allies. Try a joint promotion with another marketer: Pace Picante sauce and Velveeta cheese often team up.

- Improve your weaponry. How?

  - Bring in flanker products.

  - Increase the frequency of use by current customers.

  - Keep the backing of your distributors with many trade promotions.

  - Distribute intensively.

  - Use mass media optimally.

  - Stress brand differentiation and benefits.

  - Stimulate brand-switching to your products.

  - Heavier price competition is OK, but avoid price wars at all costs to maintain profitability.

- Don't retreat behind a drawbridge and moat and prepare boiling water to pour over the walls of your castle when your enemy attacks. That's a passive defense. If you have this *garrison mentality,* you'll probably use it. My advice — don't do it! Instead, do these things:

  - Maintain active marketing patrols.

  - Keep probing for your enemy's weaknesses.

  - Continue your aggression against your enemy.

The Decline Stage: Retreat Tactics

The Situation

- A permanently declining demand for all brands, including yours — definitely Battleground 2 or 4 (probably 4).

- Fewer competitors, fewer (and older) customers.

- Prices are stable, but sales decline.

- Your objective may be to:

  - Leave the battlefield to conserve your resources.

  - Replace a current product with a new one.

  - Reduce a beachhead that never grew much.

Retreat Tactics

- Be careful of the morale of your troops — it's lowest during a retreat.

- Maintain tight control over your troops' attitude so that withdrawal doesn't turn into a rout.

- Keep your enemy off-balance while you retreat, but don't spend too much to do it — a contested withdrawal, not a scorched earth policy.

- Reduce expenditures and milk your brand.

- Continually prune your product line to items returning *direct* profit only.

- Get rid of not only your Losers but also the Dogs you've come to know and love over the years.

- Keep profits up by avoiding the temptation to lower your price.

- Forget about market share and your ego, even if you used to be king of the hill.

- Lower advertising and sales promotion guns to levels needed to retain hardcore loyals only.

- Let your product coast on its own merits.

- Phase out unprofitable outlets.

- Allow intelligence gathering to deteriorate.

- Eventually, abandon the marketplace. Chess players resign

instead of playing through to the end of an obviously lost game. Here's what Clausewitz said: "When a battle proceeding disadvantageously is arrested before its conclusion, its minus result on our side not only disappears from the account but also becomes the foundation for a greater victory."

- Finally, choose one of the five decline tactics:

  - Increase your investment if you're still an optimist. Why? To dominate or get a good competitive position.

  - Hold your investment level steady until uncertainties about the industry are resolved.

  - Decrease your investment posture selectively by saying goodbye to unpromising customer groups, while simultaneously strengthening your investment posture within the lucrative segments of enduring customer demands.

  - Harvest (or milk) your investment to recover cash quickly, regardless of the resulting investment posture.

  - Divest the business quickly by disposing of its assets as advantageously as possible.

The Rejuvenation Stage: Tactics to Attack a Different Battleground

The Situation

- Your never-say-die spirit has led you to find new uses for your brand.

- Customers respond to your communication of these new uses, but their response is not as great as it was during earlier stages of the life cycle.

- Your objective should be: Continue your profitable business in a different market.

- Your objective should not be: Feed your ego. It's OK, though, to feel this way: "I'm not going to let my enemy grind me down after all I've built up. I'll continue my once-profitable business in a different market."

Tactics to Attack a Different Battleground

- Announce new uses with a lot of public relations gimmickry and propaganda — create a major publicity event.

- Use marketing weapons cautiously. Remember, you're spending at a much lower level now, so you can't do as much as before. For example, when Warner-Lambert resurrected Corn Huskers Lotion, they went with a low-key, low-cost radio campaign — one market at a time until, little by little, they covered the entire nation.

- Once again, target early adopters and dealers in your promotion to build high awareness levels.

- Use them as commandos to gain brand acceptance and keep distribution.

- Use speed and surprise.

- Here are some less dramatic examples of rejuvenation:

  - The periodic facelifts given to Betty Crocker by General Mills (more than ten different facelifts since 1936)

  - Putting the two pudgy Campbell's kids on a diet so that Campbell's Soup could appeal more to the yogurt-and-vitamin crowd

  - A slimmer Aunt Jemima looking toward you from the pancake mix box

  - Slimming and putting clothes on the formerly topless winged goddess Psyche on the White Rock beverage labels. In 1894, she was 5 feet 4 inches tall, 140 pounds, with measurements of 37-27-38. In 1975, when she put on a top, she became 5 feet 8 inches tall, 118 pounds, with measurements of 35-24-34. How standards of sexiness have changed!

- Don't forget to rejuvenate your tired sales force, too. How? Through *personal* leadership once again, with many field trips — but stay within your modest budget. Why get in unnecessary trouble with your bosses?

- Remember Sun Tzu's advice on how to turn a desperate situation to your advantage. He said:

  - Soldiers naturally resist when they're surrounded, so throw them into a position from which there is no escape, and they'll prefer death to running away.

  - Soldiers lose the sense of fear when they are in extremely desperate situations and they know there is no hope. They fight more valiantly when they are not afraid.

  - Soldiers will stand firm when there is no way to get to a place of refuge.

  - Soldiers will fight the enemy in vicious hand-to-hand combat when they are in the middle of the enemy's land.

- On the other hand, if things get too desperate, your sales reps will desert and go work for another company, quite possibly your enemy — and they'll take all your secret information with them.

Moving Forward: Your Plan of Action

Digest what you've learned here. When you're back in the office behind a desk, or when you're in the field contacting customers and negotiating with them, your mindset will guide you into choosing one strategy over another, one tactic over another. You probably have either a guerrilla mindset or the mindset of a Big Dog. No matter if you're a guerrilla or a Big Dog, I wish you well. Like Star Trek's Mr. Spock always said, "Live long and prosper." Living long is beyond the scope of this book. Prosperity comes from applying what you've learned so far and what you'll learn in the rest of this book.

Winning Business Warfare the Guerrilla Way

GETTING BIG BY THINKING SMALL

Guerrilla warfare is most suitable for products and services in Business Battleground 4 (low attraction, low strength), as you saw in Chapter 6, page 105. That chapter's plan of action also told you that 94 percent of all products and services are in Business Battleground 4, and that guerrilla warfare tactics should be used in this Battleground. So if you're in that 94 percent category, this is an important chapter for you. Don't skip over it.

Thinking Small Is Really Thinking Big: The Sam Walton Success Story

It seems hard to believe that the world's largest and most powerful retailer, Wal-Mart, was started by a guerrilla. I think Sam Walton was the best guerrilla warrior of all time. I call him the *ultimate* guerrilla. Here's his story:

Sam owned a series of small five-and-ten-cent variety stores in northwestern Arkansas in the 1940s and 1950s. Eventually he and his brother Ben ran sixteen stores in that part of the United States — Arkansas, Missouri, and Kansas. He was losing customers to discount chain stores such as Woolco and Kmart, even though they were located in larger cities over 100 miles away. People from Bentonville, where he was headquartered, drove over dangerous winding mountain roads to go to Little Rock, Fort Smith, Springfield, Joplin, Tulsa, and Kansas City where the discount stores were located.

Sam couldn't match the chains' low prices — his stores were too small to buy in bulk. So he decided to outmaneuver them by coming up with a bold and daring idea that cost him a lot of his assets. He figured that three stores the size of his original Ben Franklin store in Bentonville would match the buying power of a smaller Woolco or Kmart. So he set up a small warehouse in the center of several small towns in Arkansas. He bought in sufficient bulk that he could match the prices of the Woolcos and Kmarts in those larger cities. He opened his first Wal-Mart in Bentonville in 1962.

What happened? The big chains ignored him. They didn't want to invade smaller cities anyway. They, like Chiang Kai-Shek in China, were too cautious to go after their enemies in the countryside. And they eventually lost the war.

Sam took advantage of the big chains' indifference and kept expanding. He set up more and more warehouses, and added more and more retail stores. He stuck to small towns.

Eventually, like Mao Tse-Tung and Le Duan, the guerrilla architect of North Viet Nam's victory over the United States and South Viet Nam, he decided to attack the large cities in force. He started in Philadelphia, and Wal-Mart there was a big winner. By then he was too big to be stopped by the big discount chains.

He began opening Wal-Marts in the outer suburbs of large cities, where Americans were moving and land was cheaper. His stores were larger than the Woolcos and Kmarts. Economies of scale. The older Woolcos and Kmarts weren't as large, clean, and attractive as the newer Wal-Marts, and they had higher rental and insurance rates. With their higher operating costs, they couldn't match Wal-Mart's efficiencies and had to charge higher prices.

Eventually Wal-Mart became the number one retailer in the world. Woolco went out of business. Kmart merged with Sears. Other big discounters went out of business, too. Anybody remember E. J. Korvette, a giant discount chain in the northeastern United States? Long gone. How about GEM? Treasure Island? Richway? Ditto.

The moral of the story: *Thinking small is actually thinking big.* Think like winners — think small! Even if you're with a big company! You'll win more.

Sam Walton and Mao Tse-Tung

The story of Sam Walton tells you why I based this chapter on the concept "Getting Big by Thinking Small." When I was professor of marketing at a university in Arkansas, I got to know Sam. He told me he had read Mao Tse-Tung's *Yu Chi Chan (Guerrilla Warfare)* and was influenced by it. So here are the 22 most powerful guerrilla weapons from Mao's 1937 book. They may be the weapons Sam Walton felt were important, too:

1. Always stay on the offensive.
2. Always stay alert so you'll see hidden opportunities to win.
3. Attack where the Big Dog is weakest.
4. Use shock and awe. How? Move suddenly, quickly, and ferociously.
5. Ambush the Big Dog. Surprise the Big Dog by attacking when and where it's unexpected.
6. Know who to avoid and when to avoid them.
7. Attack only when your forces are superior — very superior.
8. Attack only when you're certain you'll win.
9. Be more mobile, more flexible, than the Big Dog.
10. Lose your ego. Know when to withdraw. And do it, don't just think about it!
11. Retreat quickly whenever the Big Dog becomes superior. Wait for another opportunity, then attack again.
12. Confuse the Big Dog by withdrawing quickly after you win a small victory.
13. Confuse the Big Dog by spreading false information.
14. Put the Big Dog off balance. When the Big Dog thinks east, you attack from the west.
15. Take advantage of the Big Dog's rhythm when he is unsettled, and you'll win big.
16. Weaken the Big Dog. How? Disperse, harass, and exhaust the Big Dog, and disrupt supply lines and communication lines.
17. Use the Big Dog's supplies.

18. Get allies — you're an underdog, so you need help. Especially allies in the Big Dog's inner circle and in the media.

19. Go one step beyond allies. Recruit spies — somebody close to the Big Dog who holds a grudge. Spies get revenge by seeing you win.

20. Pay your spies well.

21. Don't trust your spies completely — they may be counterspies.

22. Be completely ruthless.

Guerrilla Warfare Phase One: The Early Beginnings

Mao's 22 weapons are most suitable for what I call phase one of guerrilla warfare — the early beginnings, for when you're small and underfinanced. When Mao wrote *Yu Chi Chan* in 1937 he was still a traditional guerrilla. He was fighting the Japanese, who had invaded China in 1934. Mao didn't take power until the late 1940s. The Japanese were no longer the enemy between 1945 and 1949 — Chiang Kai-Shek, the President of China, was. That's when Mao modified his tactics and moved into phase two of guerrilla warfare — direct, strong, decisive attacks. You'll want to move into phase two quickly if you want to win badly enough. If you were content with being small, you wouldn't have bought this book.

Decisive Attacks

When Mao said "Only great battles can produce great results," he was predicting his own future. He didn't win his total victory in mainland China until 1949, when he attacked Chiang Kai-Shek's Kuomintang (Nationalist) forces in full-scale combat.

Le Duan, the architect of North Vietnam's defeat of South Vietnam in the mid-1970s, used his allies, the Vietcong guerrillas, to harass and demoralize the South Vietnam army for over 20 years, but the Vietcong didn't win that war for North Vietnam. That war was won only when Le Duan marshaled battle-strength North Vietnam regulars and attacked the South in brutal, full-scale combat as Mao had done in China thirty years earlier.

Guerrilla Warfare Phase Two: Direct, Strong, Decisive Attacks

If you want to win badly enough, you won't want to stay in phase one of guerrilla warfare too long. You'll be too ambitious to stay underfinanced and small. And so once you, the guerrilla gnat, have sufficiently weakened your giant enemy, it's time to move into phase two — a direct attack, using full battle strength. Your objective: Gain a decisive victory against your foes, the market leaders.

We already know, intuitively, that better price, quality, reliability, and service help increase market shares, all else being equal. But that's not specific enough. You bought this book to learn something new and valuable. So here are 21 tactics you can use to win your marketing battles, along with examples. As you read each of them, ask yourself if your company can use the tactic or not.

1. Improve your services.

   - Avis tried to convince the public it was trying harder than Hertz in its service. It got more customers, but Avis never did become number one.

   - Singapore Airlines stresses the in-flight services offered by its *Singapore Girl* flight attendants to economy class passengers.

2. Use creative distribution methods.

   - Timex introduced the idea of selling watches through mass-merchandise channels instead of through jewelry stores.

   - Amway developed the multilevel merchandising (pyramid) plan and gave it respectability.

   - Be careful, though. Love Cosmetics failed when it decided to sell only through drugstores, ignoring the large department-store market for cosmetics. Anybody remember that loser?

3. Buy out competitors. G. Heileman Brewing Company has bought out such firms as Carling, Blatz, Wiedemann, Rainier, Falls City, and many other brewers over the years to become a powerful number-three company in that industry. It specialized in regional brands that are Big Dogs in their geographic markets. Heileman was bought by Stroh's and now is brewed by Pabst.

4. Spend heavily on advertising. A rule of thumb is that you have to out-spend your competitor three-to-one. Guerrillas usually don't have that kind of money, and the Big Dog will retaliate quickly.

   - Hunt spent $6.4 million per year to Heinz's $3.4 million per year in trying to become the number-one ketchup. This was less than a two-to-one ratio. At that time, Heinz had a 27 percent market share and Hunt had a 19 percent share. Hunt didn't achieve its goal. A few months into Hunt's spending spree, Heinz had increased its market share to over 40 percent.

5. Apply superior technology and innovation. In the battle of Crecy in 1346, King Henry V of Britain beat Europe's number-one army, the French, with a new invention, the longbow. It was six times faster than the crossbow the French used, and it could penetrate armor, which was beyond the capability of the crossbow. Some examples of superior technology in marketing include the following:

   - The Xerox machine was a quantum leap in technology over film and carbon paper.

   - Polaroid's instant photography was also a tremendous leap in technology over Kodak's film when it was first introduced. But Polaroid stopped innovating and is a minor player today.

   - Crest toothpaste's seal of approval from the American Dental Association enabled it to knock off the number-one Colgate. It's still number one.

   - Yamaha motorcycle's starter button enabled it to knock off BSA, Triumph, and the entire British motorcycle industry, which had a 70 percent market share in the United States when Yamaha started its invasion of the American market.

6. Lower your price. This may not always work, because price is the easiest — and quickest — variable in the entire marketing mix for your competitors to copy. Here's when it's most likely to work:

   - When your offering is a well-established one and consumers have well-established perceptions of the expected benefits

   - When your competitors don't follow quickly

   - When the price change is a direct monetary reduction

7. Enter the private-brand and generic-brand market. So many examples, so little space. The trade journal you read probably has hundreds of examples.

8. Offer a prestige product at a higher price. Mercedes overtook Cadillac that way.

9. Offer a prestige product at a lower price. Dangerous because eventually you have to raise your prices, and your customers will abandon you. Google Tower Records and see what I mean. It's not around anymore. But it did pretty well for a lot of years.

10. Offer a proliferation of products. An expensive way to get business. Guerrillas usually don't have enough money or staying power to do this, though.

11. Be creative in your sales promotions. Avoid the run-of-the-mill predictable kinds you see around you all the time, each year (or month) at the same time. Taco Bell in Honolulu ran the same "Buy one, get one free" coupon for its Burrito Supreme and Taco Light brands in the local newspapers on the best food day in the last week of each month for more than a year. That failing Taco Bell franchise in Hawaii was eventually bought out by a true guerrilla who used several of these decisive attacks, and sales skyrocketed.

12. Use point-of-purchase materials creatively.

13. Reduce your production cost. Be a better purchasing agent. Learn how to negotiate better with suppliers. Chapter 11, pages 181–210 gives you a list of 365 powerful ways to make deals. I developed them over the years and present them in my negotiation seminars all over the world.

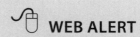 **WEB ALERT**

For ideas on how to use POP materials creatively, check out the Point-of-Purchase Advertising Institute at popai.com and the Promotional Marketing Association at pmalink.org.

14. Outsource your work — if it can be done without a decline in quality.

15. Obtain more modern production equipment.

16. See if you can lower your labor costs, perhaps by hiring consultants who are known to be efficiency experts.

17. Run your company like a small business, and watch every penny.

18. Expand from a class market to a mass market. Miller Beer (formerly positioned as the "champagne of bottled beer") did this when Philip Morris bought them out. It's a powerhouse today. But the once-upon-a-time-guerrilla Miller used Big-Dog money to expand its market. It couldn't have done it on its own.

19. Come up with a new use for an old product. Remember the Arm & Hammer Baking Soda example in Chapter 7, page 115. But what about regional soft drink marketers? They're missing the boat — cola can be used to remove rust from cars. And small coffee companies? I haven't seen any campaigns that say "Add coffee to add flavor to spaghetti sauce, to fertilize indoor plants, or to transport worms for fishing." Maybe I will if one of their executives reads this book.

20. Be the first to own a market segment that's increasing in importance, so that you'll be hard to dislodge. Two examples: The Hispanic market. Aging baby boomers. Another example: The gay market, which has become loud and proud. It's no longer silent and ashamed.

21. Put your local ads in national magazines to gain prestige. Media Networks Inc. caters to local advertisers, such as Baptist Medical System of Little Rock, Arkansas, who want to look like national advertisers while paying only for a targeted local market or a zip-coded section of a market. Media Networks offers nine different networks of demographically compatible magazines, where your ad will alternate from one magazine to another throughout the month. Get more info at mni.com.

The Guerrilla's Middle Ground: Follow-the-Leader Tactics

Let's recap. I call phase one of guerrilla warfare the early beginnings. Mao's 22 tactics are appropriate for this phase. I call phase two direct, strong, decisive attacks. There's a middle ground, and I call it follow-the-leader. Here's what the middle ground is all about:

Suppose you're too ambitious to be a small guerrilla but think it's too dangerous to challenge the leader head-on. You don't really want to adopt a chicken or falcon risk profile. What can you do? Some companies think that following the market leader makes a lot of sense. It makes sense in industries such as chemicals and steel. These industries are capital-intensive. There is very little they can do to differentiate their products, services, or image. Price wars are likely whenever a firm is greedy enough to disrupt the status quo.

In these kinds of industries, market shares are rather stable, which indicates that most firms decide against attacking each other to gain extra market-share points. Instead, most firms try to do nothing that will rock the boat, and this usually means copying the leader in the industry. The key objective is to not create competitive retaliation. When many firms do this, it's called conscious parallel action. Big words for a simple concept. And there are three very simple tactics you can use. They work. Try them out and see.

1. Follow closely. Copy the Big Dog as much as possible without radically blocking the leader. In brainstorming sessions with my clients, I call this me-too-ism. Sometimes, I call it parasite marketing because these firms hope to live off the leader's investments without investing in any R&D themselves.

2. Follow at a distance. Copy what the Big Dog does in terms of major market and product innovations, general price levels, and distribution — but still keep some important differences. Sometimes these firms grow by acquiring smaller companies in the industry (see phase two, tactic three on page 135). The market leader usually won't retaliate because the distant follower interferes as little as possible with the leader's plans.

3. Follow selectively. Follow the Big Dog closely in some areas and act independently in others. A study I read recently said that many companies with less than half the market share of the industry's leader had a five-year average return on equity that was larger than the industry's median. Therefore, this tactic can be a very successful one.

Some successful market followers include Burroughs (business equipment) and Crown Cork & Seal (packaging).

Moving Forward: Your Plan of Action

No matter which set of underdog tactics you pick — phase one (early beginnings), phase two (decisive attacks), or the middle ground (follow-the-leader) — don't think it will be an easy trip to king-of-the-hill status. Conducting a guerrilla campaign can be quite expensive. It's not just a low-resource tactic most suitable to financially weak challengers. It's expensive because, eventually, guerrilla warfare must be backed up by a much stronger attack if you want to become number one. Mao Tse-Tung knew that and he eventually conquered mainland China when he got out of his guerrilla costume and into his field-army uniform. Will the guerrillas in your industry eventually conquer their enemies? Will they stay guerrillas forever? Or will they give up and disappear from the scene? I hope you won't be a casualty. You won't if you make a conscious effort to influence the outcome of the struggle.

And if you're a leader, don't let the guerrillas grow too strong. There are many examples of guerrillas graduating into the big leagues. So let's leave guerrilla tactics now and learn how a dominant company can stop guerrillas and other challengers dead in their tracks and protect its number-one position. Turn the page and read Chapter 9, "Winning Business Warfare the Big Dog's Way."

Winning Business Warfare the Big Dog's Way

This chapter will appeal to everybody, because everybody wants to be a Big Dog. Guerrillas will learn how to get inside the mind of Big Dogs. That's the first step in replacing them as kings of the hill. Big Dogs will recognize themselves, maybe even laugh at themselves self-consciously. And they'll learn how to keep their Big-Dog status intact.

Six Kinds of Big Dog: Which One Are You?

Management consulting firm Arthur D. Little said there are six competitive positions in every industry. Which one is your company in?

- *Dominant firms.* They're the biggest of the Big Dogs. They control the behavior of their competitors. They have the largest choice of strategic and tactical options.

- *Strong firms.* They're the second largest Big Dogs. They can take independent action without worrying about damaging their long-term position. Regardless of what their competitors do, they can still keep that desirable position for a long, long time.

- *Firms in a favorable position.* They're Big Dogs who are still strong. They exploit their strength whenever they can. They have more opportunities to improve their position than most firms have.

- *Firms in a tenable position.* They're Big Dogs that are starting to weaken. They'll stay in business because they're performing satisfactorily. But they don't have as many opportunities to improve their positions. And they stay in business only because the dominant firm lets them. I guess dominant companies need somebody to laugh at, like the lovable sidekick in those old western movies.

- *Weak firms.* These companies aren't performing satisfactorily. They're Big Dogs that are noticeably weak. There's only a slight opportunity for them to improve. They must seize that opportunity or get out.

- *Nonviable firms.* These companies aren't performing satisfactorily. They're Big Dogs on their last legs. Because they have no opportunities to improve, they should probably get out of the industry as fast as possible.

If you're dominant, be thankful. You have the largest selection of strategic and tactical options to choose from. You're almost like a kid in a candy store — there are so many goodies around, you don't know which goodie to pick first. This chapter gives you a variety of goodies to choose from. Pick and use them wisely, because each one works best in one particular situation.

It's More Complicated Than What You Read in Chapter 6

Go back to Figure 6.3, Guerrilla Don Hendon's Four Battlegrounds of Business — *stark naked* version. It's on page 97. Remember Battleground 1? High Attraction, High Strength. There, on page 102, I gave you five general suggestions for a frontal attack:

- Stay dominant at all costs.

- Counterattack any upstart.

- Pursue and smash *any* significant enemy ruthlessly as a warning to new enemies who may be attracted to this market.

- Don't give up control of the situation. Stay on the attack, maintaining your momentum.

- Don't be predictable. Keep your enemy off-balance.

And remember Battleground 2? Low Attraction, High Strength. On page 103 I gave you five general suggestions for defending what you already have:

- Make your enemies *think* your position is stronger than it is by keeping in control of the situation, not abandoning your leadership, staying on the attack, and keeping your momentum. Maintain an aura of vicious invulnerability.

- Use the BCG's hold strategy and preserve your market share.

- Keep a lot of money in reserve so you can counterattack as viciously as possible with a mobile strike force.

- Increase profitability not by drastic economizing but by cutting costs selectively if necessary. Drastic economizing will weaken you.

- Seek opportunities to demoralize your enemies whenever possible. After all, you've got the cash flow to do it.

Those ten suggestions aren't nearly enough. Here are two checklists that will help you stay king of the hill:

- The product/target market checklist
- The growth checklist

The Product/Target Market Checklist

☑ **Penetrate your markets: Increase the use of old products in old markets.**

- Get your present customers to use more — the easiest and quickest way.

- Increase the unit of purchase. Change from 6-packs to 12-packs, from 12-packs to a case.

- Build in more product obsolescence.

- Advertise other uses for your product.

- Make the container opening larger so that your buyers will use it up faster.

☑ **Go after your competitors' customers: Get them to switch to you.**

- Exploit weaknesses in your competitors' offerings.
- Make sharper brand differentiations.
- Promote more heavily.
- Cut prices if your target market is price-conscious.
- Raise prices if your target market is prestige-conscious.

☑ **Go after non-users with demographics similar to your users, if there are many of them.**

- Induce trial by sampling, price inducements, easy financing, etc. Use your creative imagination here. Re-read Chapter 5.
- Advertise other new uses for your product.
- Use new advertising media.
- Use different pricing tactics than you used before.
- Try different distributors.

☑ **Develop markets: Sell your old products in new markets.**

- Use new distribution channels.
- Make handling your account very profitable to them.
- Don't alienate your present likely distributors, though.

☑ **Move into new geographic markets.**

- Expand regionally.
- Expand nationally.
- Expand internationally.

☑ **Develop products: Introduce new products in old markets.**

- Use a completely different technology.
  - Increase R&D expenditures.
  - Raid key technical talent from other companies.
- Increase product proliferation. Introduce many brands aimed at slightly different market segments that don't cannibalize your present brands.
  - Introduce fighting brands with low prices.
  - Introduce prestige brands with high prices.

- Develop quality variations in your basic product offering.
  - Go after the prestige market with a high-quality product.
  - Go after the mass market with an average-quality product.
  - Go after the disinterested, price-conscious market with a low-quality product.
- Develop new product features.
  - Consider changing the dimensions: larger, smaller, longer, shorter, thicker, thinner, deeper, shallower.
  - Consider changing the quantity: more, less, change proportions, fractionate, join something, add something to it, combine with something else.
  - Consider changing the order: arrangement, precedence, beginning.
  - Consider changing the time element: faster, slower, longer, shorter.
  - Consider a change in character: stronger, weaker, altered, reversed, resilient, cheaper, more expensive, add color, change color.
  - Consider changing the form: animated, speeded, slowed, directed, lifted, lowered.
  - Consider changing the state or condition: hotter, colder, harder, softer, open or closed, disposable, solidified, liquefied, pulverized, wetter, drier, effervesced, lighter, heavier.
  - Consider adapting the use to a new market: men, women, children, old, handicapped.

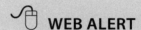

WEB ALERT

Go to GuerrillaDon.com to download a comprehensive, 122-question checklist on developing new product features. Several thousand words, several million ideas!

☑ **Diversify: Introduce new products in new markets.**

- Bring out products that give you technological and marketing synergies because they're compatible with your present product line.
  - Do market research to find the optimal product mix.
  - Get help from your production people and engineers, but make sure they know what marketing's all about first.
- Bring out products that are completely unrelated to your line, markets, and technology.
  - Do market research to find out what your distributors and final customers really want.
  - Spend the money necessary to make this new venture a success.

The Growth Checklist

☑ **Acquire familiar firms — grow within your industry by buying out other companies.**

- Do this only if you have a lot of knowledge of the company, if a unique opportunity comes along, and if there are strong barriers to internal development.
  - Buy out suppliers.
  - Buy out wholesalers.
  - Buy out retailers.
  - Buy out competitors.
  - Buy out some combination of the above.

☑ **Acquire unfamiliar firms — grow by buying out companies in other industries.**

- Do it if a unique opportunity comes along and if there are strong barriers to internal development. But be careful —you may not have enough knowledge to make a good decision. Once again, buy out suppliers, wholesalers, retailers, manufacturers, or some combination of the above.

☑ **Develop internally — get bigger all by yourself.**

- Do this if you're barred by the government from acquiring other firms, if you can't buy out companies because the field is too new, or if you want to get firsthand experience in the new field itself.

  - Spend enough on research and development.

  - Raid other companies for key experienced personnel.

☑ **Think outside of the box — grow outside your industry.**

- Act like a conglomerate by going completely outside your marketing system.

  - Rely heavily on the advice of your financial and tax experts.

  - Have enough financial leverage to get the job done. Try a leveraged buyout.

Moving Forward: Your Plan of Action

It's pretty nice to be strong enough to be in Battleground 1 or Battleground 2, isn't it? You're king of the hill and have a lot of resources behind you, so you'll probably be a winner for a long time. You worry a little about getting a new boss who doesn't understand how important you and your contributions are to the company, though. But right now, you're in charge of a winner, and you're probably a winner in your personal life, too.

To stay a winner, don't be complacent. Always stay hungry. Emulate Samuel Gompers, the founder of the American Federation of Labor over 100 years ago. A newspaper reporter asked him, "What does the American labor movement want?" He gave a one-word answer. "More." His remark found its way into American history texts. So always want more. Don't be complacent. Don't use the passive defense you read about in Chapter 7, page 125.

If you've follow the principles outlined in this book so far and have learned how to blend the four Ps of the marketing mix in the proper manner, it'll be very hard to ever become a loser. The next chapter builds on the Marketing 101 course you took in college. It covers the four Ps of marketing from the viewpoint of the successful Business Warrior. Don't skip over it because you got an "A" in Marketing 101. It's not a rehash of that course. Instead, you'll read about *unique* ways of using the four Ps. While reading the chapter, make sure you think about how you'll blend your four Ps together at each of the stages of the product life cycle. You need to think about these things because chances are high that your brands will be in each of the four Business Battlegrounds and in each of the six product life cycle stages before your career as a successful Business Warrior is over and you retire as a big success. Start building your legacy today!

Hidden Gems You Didn't Learn in Marketing 101

I got my BBA, MBA, and PhD degrees in marketing. When I was growing up in Laredo, Texas, our family was prosperous because it owned an outdoor advertising company. I took it over. Sold it for big bucks. After that I was a sales rep, sales manager, and brand manager. I've consulted for hundreds of firms — mostly outside the United States — in several areas of marketing, specializing in international negotiating and dealmaking. What I'm going to tell you here is street-smart knowledge — definitely not the same old 4 Ps your old marketing professor stressed in Marketing 101. The unique topics, combined with my insights and experience, will make you a big winner in business. You'll be a very successful Business Warrior. Look over the fifteen topics you'll read about. Read the one that interests you the most. Then go to the one that interests you the second most. And so forth. I'll bet you read them all. And, yes, I've got a big ego. Most winners have big egos. You're probably a winner or well on your way to being a winner, so I'll bet you have a big ego, too. Enjoy it, make a lot of money, retire early, and keep your mind busy managing your profitable investments. Play a lot of golf. Have fun.

Here's what you'll learn in this chapter: You'll start with price, because it's the easiest and quickest variable in the marketing mix to change. We'll cover three topics:

- How to recognize when a price war is about to erupt.

- How to win a price war.

- When you should charge high prices and when you should charge low prices.

Next, product wars. We'll cover two topics:

- Why new products fail and what you can do about it.

- How to choose a great brand name.

Next, promotion wars. We'll cover six topics this time, because advertising, personal selling, and sales promotion are all part of the promotion mix:

- How to use ad media, from the business warrior's viewpoint.

- How to evaluate the effectiveness of your promotion campaign.

- Advice on holding sales contests.

- How to engage in personal selling — think and act like a consultant, not like a sales rep.

- How to choose your ad agency.

- Why ad agencies get fed up and drop clients.

Finally, place (channels of distribution) wars. We'll cover three topics:

- How to choose your distributors.

- Complaints about distributors.

- What distributors want to know about your product.

At the end of the chapter, you'll see an in-basket case study, The Business Warrior's Worksheet, which you can do by yourself or in groups. It will give you immediate feedback about whether your strategies and tactics were good or bad.

Price Wars

Nobody wins in a price war. Profits drop for all companies. And consumers also lose in the long run. Why? Because weaker companies are bled to death, there are fewer sources of supply, and prices go up. It's very important to avoid a price war, if at all possible.

What can you do about price wars? Two things:

- Recognize the early warning signs of the price war to come.

- Be a winner, not just a survivor.

How to Recognize When a Price War is About to Erupt

These are the early warning signs of a price war:

- There is excess capacity in your industry.

- One of your competitors has a much lower cost structure than anybody else. It will be the company that starts the price war. So watch that company carefully.

- There are many price-sensitive customers who are quick to react to a price cut. This includes both distributors and final consumers.

- The product is no longer differentiated. In the eyes of distributors and final consumers, it's now a me-too product, a commodity.

- One of the companies in your industry strongly believes it can shut out or drive out one of the other companies and wants to try to do it. It's one sign of an ego trip.

- One of your competitors wants to buy a position in the marketplace, even if it costs a lot of time and money. It's another sign of an ego trip.

- One of your competitors has heavy financial resources behind it. This allows that company to weather the storm without too many problems.

- The market is large enough to fight over.

- The market is a mature one. Prices are usually cut toward the end of the maturity stage of the product life cycle.

- There is a general belief in your industry that a price cut may expand the total market for everybody.

- Somebody in your industry is making excessive profits, and you and most of your competitors know who this company is.

- There is at least one slow, weak competitor that can be hurt the most. You and most of your competitors know who this is. All the stronger firms will do things to get rid of this weakling so they can take over its market share. Watch out if you're the slow, weak competitor.

- Most companies in your industry share a general belief that order will eventually replace the chaos of a price war. So the company that begins the price war doesn't fear any long-term consequences. And neither will the firms that enthusiastically enter the war later on.

How to Win a Price War

How can you not only survive a price war but win big at the end? Here are four suggestions:

- Make accurate guesses about the future. Remember, one or more of the firms in the price war may have a lower cost structure. The firm that started the war probably enjoys that lower cost structure. You should use marketing intelligence to obtain cost data from your competitors. If you don't know how much it's costing them to manufacture and market their products, you'll probably make wrong guesses about their future actions and about when the price war will end.

- Look very closely at your product. Is it a commodity? Has it lost its distinctiveness in the minds of the public? If so, you need to do something about it. Make it distinctive again. If you don't do this, you won't be able to emphasize other areas of the marketing mix very much, and you'll always seem to be in one money-losing price war after the other.

- Keep your profits up in a price war. How? Look for market segments that aren't price sensitive. They may be hard to find, though. If you're in many geographic markets, widely scattered all over the country or all over the globe, you're lucky. You may be able to milk those segments during the price war to keep your cash flow coming.

- Stay in control — try to be your industry's price leader. The price leader has to keep leading at all times, or the leadership will pass to its competitors. It's especially important to lead the way in price changes because price is the quickest and easiest weapon to change in your marketing arsenal. Price is the Business Warrior's first major weapon — and the most visible weapon, too.

When You Should Charge High Prices and When You Should Charge Low Prices

Figure 10.1 shows the differences between high-price and low-price strategies. Two warnings: First, this applies only in nations with high unit labor costs (definitely not India). Second, these are rules-of-thumb — in other words, this is what most marketers do. But just because most marketers do this, you may or may not want to do the same. Your situation may be very different. And when you really want to start a price war, what this list says won't matter to you. Show this list to other marketing executives in your company and discuss it. It will generate a lot of heated arguments, but it'll also serve a valuable purpose — your group will re-think the essentials of pricing tactics. All of you will get back to basics.

Product Wars

Why New Products Fail and What You Can Do About it

These reasons happen over and over. Have they happened to your brands?

- No real benefit is delivered. Make sure your customers perceive — and actually receive — important benefits, or you won't succeed.

- Competitors deliver unexpectedly heavy responses. Position your product carefully so you won't be vulnerable to competitive reactions. This means developing a major product advantage and positioning it before your competitors occupy that position.

- There are changes in the market. Carefully monitor your market through the design, test, launch, and mature phases of development. How? By designing a top-notch environmental sensor system.

Charge Low Price If Factor Is:	Factors to Be Considered	Charge High Price If Factor Is:
Slow	Technological change	Rapid
Short	Channels of distribution	Long
Few or none	Extras that come with the product	Many
Mass-produced	Manufacturing process	Custom-made
Intensive	Market coverage	Selective
Large	Market share	Small
Mature	Market — stage of market	New
Long-lived	Product obsolescence	Short-lived
Commodity	Product type	Proprietary
Single-use	Product versatility	Multiple-use
Capital-intensive	Production	Labor-intensive
Short	Product life — how long customers will use it	Long
Long-term	Profit perspective	Short-term
Little	Promotion — amount	Much
Much	Promotion's contribution to the line	Little
Fast-moving	Turnover	Slow-moving

Figure 10.1. Differences between low-price and high-price strategies

- There's a forecasting error. Remember, most errors happen early. Your forecasts become more accurate as your new product moves through the development process. Rough forecasts first occur at the design phase. They are refined by pre-test market analysis. They are finalized at the test market stage. And they are monitored during the launch.

- Goals aren't clearly defined. Often, you have conflicts of interest within your company's operations. Sometimes a few jealous empire-builders will try to sabotage a new product launch to make themselves look good by comparison. How many of you have worked for a company that introduced a "new and improved" formula only because they needed something to hype at their regional sales meetings. I have. Eventually we found out that the formula was new, but it didn't perform as well as the existing brand. So watch out for these trouble-makers who want to see you fail.

- The product is a me-too product — neither new nor different. Use creative methods (see Chapter 5, pages 79 – 89) to generate real advantages and uniquely position your product — make it as different as possible from your competitors' products. Make sure your unique features are important to your middlemen and final consumers. Make sure they are evident in your advertising and in the way your product performs in use.

- Distributors provide poor support. Make sure that you reward your distributors so they'll be more likely to push your product. Test your product concept with distributors to see if they'll stock and support it even before you market-test it in the field.

- The new product proposal is oversold. Overenthusiasm can blind you to market realities. Is the new product somebody's baby? If so, it's very hard to tell someone that their baby isn't going to make it and they should drop the project. And you're not seen as creative in many companies unless you're introducing a lot of new products. Too much pressure for new products isn't good either. I think 3M went too far by calling every new size and color of its Post-it Notes a new product. What do you think?

- The product is a poor match for the company. Do research to see if the market matches the unique competencies of your company. And do this early in the new product development process.

- The product is poorly positioned. Fill the right gap before anybody else does. See Chapter 4, pages 65 – 75.

- There's not enough return on investment. Make sure you pay careful attention to profitability before you go too far in your development process.

- The market is too small. First, you've got to know the competitive boundaries and the market's growth. And you've got to test the concept and the product. This will help you generate an accurate forecast when you're designing the product. Make final checks on the size of the market in each of your test markets.

- Product development is rushed. Your boss puts pressure on you. This makes you bring the product to market too early. Be careful about departures from timetables.

- Product development is delayed. If you're a perfectionist or a procrastinator, you bring the product to market too late. Once again, be careful about departures from timetables.

Here are ten other things you can do. These have to do with your personal qualities and talents. Make sure that:

- You are very familiar with your competitors' product development practices.

- You are able to break away from your past practices, concepts, and viewpoints if necessary.

- You have the technical knowledge and skills needed to succeed.

- You know how to plan a successful product development program.

- You know how to choose a good brand name.

- You can differentiate between good packaging and bad packaging.

- You understand all the problems involved.

- You have enough time to spend on your product and don't over-extend yourself.

- You have a broad view of your product development program.

- You can get rid of your negative thinking and stop procrastinating — your failure to recognize a good opportunity in time means lost opportunities, perhaps even the loss of your job.

Finally, make sure that:

- Your company protects proprietary product ideas.
- Your company has sufficient facilities for product development.

How to Choose a Great Brand Name

A great brand name. That's what you're shooting for. How can you be sure that your new product is named properly? This checklist will help you. It has lots of examples. Come up with your own.

1. Use an attention-getter, such as My Sin perfume, Old Smuggler Blended Scotch Whisky, and Twenty Mule Team Borax. And don't forget Smooth Moves herbal tea with laxative ingredients.

2. Use celebrities, politicians, and people in the news, but make sure they're long-lasting. Billy Beer (named after former U.S. President Jimmy Carter's brother) is no longer around. On the other hand, Baby Ruth candy bars (named after President Taft's daughter Ruth in the early 1900s or after 1920s baseball star Babe Ruth, depending on who you believe) are still popular in the United States. In Australia, Pavlova, a fruit pie with a meringue crust, is a very popular dessert. It was named after Russian ballet great Pavlova, who died in 1931. Watch out, though. Today's popular celebrity may embarrass you tomorrow. Examples: Lance Armstrong, Tiger Woods, Lindsay Lohan, and Michael Phelps.

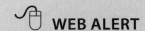

WEB ALERT

Send your brand name ideas to me at DonHendon1@aol.com. I'll post the best responses I get on GuerrillaDon.com.

3. On your label, embellish your brand name with some design to give it class. For example, Royal Dutch Shell, an oil company, features a distinctive yellow seashell on a bright red/orange background for its logo. Xerox had a red capital "X" dominate its logo for 40 years, but in 2008 launched a new logo with a stylized lower-case "x" to position the firm an an approachable, 21st century firm.

4. Is the name distinctive? Kodak is a very distinctive name. So is Disney. Fuji isn't (in Japan). Neither is Universal Studios.

5. What do you want your company's long-term position in the market to be? Is your brand named after a currently popular fad? If you want a permanent position, names such as Sputnik and Disco are not good, but they would be OK if you want only a temporary position.

6. Use geographic connotations. Lone Star advertises itself everywhere as the national beer of Texas, although most Americans already know the Lone Star State is Texas's nickname. Many beer manufacturers throughout the world use German-sounding brand names, such as Bohemia in Mexico.

7. Does your company have an image problem that a new name can help solve? Perhaps you should try a high-technology-sounding name if you're perceived as a stick-in-the-mud firm. Or use numbers for modernity, such as Trac II.

8. Make sure your brand's name doesn't insult or irritate a specific market. Yves St. Laurent's very expensive Opium perfume isn't purchased much by Chinese-Americans, perhaps because they think of opium as something that was forced upon their culture by outsiders. One of the best-selling toothpastes in Southeast Asia, Darkie, would not go over well in the United States for obvious reasons, but since it didn't insult Asians, there were no negative connotations to its name there. Still, the Hong Kong-based manufacturer gave in to protests from the United States, evn though it was not sold there. It changed its name to Darlie. And it removed the stereotypical black minstrel man with a top hat from its label and replaced it with a racially-ambiguous man with a top hat.

9. Can the name you picked be used legally in other nations? Some brand names are already trademarked overseas. In some nations, entrepreneurs read American trade journals and trademark new brand names from the United States, knowing that the American company might eventually try to introduce its brand in the entrepreneur's nation. If that happened, the American firm would have to pay ransom in order to use its trade name. In Australia, Hardee's Restaurants (the American name) called itself Hartee's to get around a trademark violation. Many people register website names in anticipation of selling them to firms later on.

10. Does the name you pick have negative connotations in other nations? Chevrolet's Nova automobile couldn't be sold in Spanish-speaking nations because *no va* means *it doesn't go.* On the other hand, the Bimbo brand of bread and snack foods is big in Mexico and other Latin American nations. The word is a combination of *bingo* and *Bambi*—innocent, clildlike associations were felt to fit the brand image the company wanted to build. It has expanded into the United States using the same name, even though *bimbo* means *easy woman* in English. Because there are so many Hispanics in the United States, it's been very successful here. However, not many of its customers in the United States are non-Hispanics.

11. Try to be funny. It's often memorable. Successful examples: Carl's Pane in the Glass (window repairs), Sew What! (alterations), and Pita Pan (restaurant).

12. Use a price connotation if you're stressing price. There are many examples, including Job Lot Bargain Stores, Family Dollar, 99 Cents Store—and the Ritz Hotel.

13. Is your product's name going to have to carry a major part of the promotion burden? If so, and if advertising dollars are short, use a very descriptive name. Example: Dunkin' Donuts.

14. What's your brand's basic role or purpose, beyond providing protection against encroachment and distinguishing it from other brands? If your brand name is going to be used to help position your product, then names such as Close-Up, Cover Girl, and Wear-Ever are good. If it's just used for identification, names such as Baskin-Robbins and Smucker's are okay. Baskin-Robbins and Smucker's reflect the names of founders of those firms but, like Kodak, are not aesthetically pleasing. *Volkswagen* means *the people's car* in German, and *Tatung* means *great commonwealth* in Chinese. Tatung is one of Taiwan's largest manufacturers of consumer products. Those are good names. On the other hand, although *Volvo* means *I roll* in Latin, how many people speak Latin today? Volvo seems too cerebral to me, but it sells very well in Sweden, its home country, and throughout the world.

15. Consider the physical and sensory qualities of your brand name.

   - Is it easy to pronounce, recognize, spell? Crest toothpaste is.

   - Does it suggest product qualities, such as action? Spic and Span detergent does.

   - Does it suggest something about the product's benefits? Simmons' Beautyrest mattress brand does.

16. Try a ridiculous name, such as Con Agra's Screaming Yellow Zonkers, which was recently re-introduced. Hershey Foods markets a candy bar called Whatchamacallits. And what about Dr Pepper? Some critics said its name sounded like a chili-flavored medicine. Those critics said that the slow growth the soft drink experienced for many years outside its southern stronghold was due to its name. When it repositioned itself, emphasizing its unique taste (not its weird name), it became the number five soft drink in the United States.

17. The word *The* tends to give a name more dignity or stature. Which sounds more prestigious, *The New York Times* or *New York Times*? The University of Texas system insists on its employees using *The* to make sure that Texans know it's *The* state university.

18. Use a name that can serve as a verb. Midas Mufflers did this when they talked about Midasizing your car. Kroger supermarkets' advertising has been urging shoppers to go Krogering for many years.

19. Are you planning to use the new product as a bridgehead to a line of products in the new category? If so, pick a name that doesn't limit you. Liquid-Plumr is a limited name (it unplugs drains). This name could never be used for a laxative. Forget about brand extensions here.

Promotion Wars

How to Use Ad Media, from the Business Warrior's Viewpoint

You're the marketing manager, the commander-in-chief. You've got all kinds of resources at your disposal — artillery, air force, infantry, armor, and airborne.

- Artillery = outdoor advertising
- Air force = network TV
- Infantry = consumer magazines and newspapers
- Armor = radio
- Airborne = direct mail and targeted e-mails

Blend them together the right way, and you'll beat the hell out of your competitors! This is how you can do it:

1. Start off with a thirty-day outdoor showing (artillery) to soften up your target market, followed by thirteen weeks of network TV (air force) to deliver a knockout blow to your competitors.

2. After you've established your position through network TV, use newspapers and consumer magazines (infantry), along with radio (armor) for six months to hold the position you've occupied.

3. Finally, use a thirty-day outdoor showing (artillery) again as a bridge to your next campaign. Of course, use direct mail and targeted e-mails (airborne) as needed.

An artillery attack precedes an air force and infantry attack to soften up the opposition. It has a heavy weight in a rather small geographic area. If you buy enough gross rating points from the outdoor plant operator, you can hit everybody in a given area with a short teaser message that makes your target market eager for the forthcoming messages in your main attack. And you can buy tons of GRPs, because outdoor offers you the cheapest cost-per-thousand of any major ad medium. Its impact, although short term, is enormous, because close to 95 percent of all people in the United States go outdoors at least once a day. And most of them pass by billboards.

National advertisers use network TV delivered by satellite or cable to hit their target with enormous weight in a large geographic area in a minimum amount of time. But it's *very, very* expensive. For example, a 30-second spot on the Super Bowl cost $3.8 million in 2013 (a 30-second spot in the first Super Bowl in 1967 cost $42,000 — a lot of money in those days). In military warfare, an air bombing attack provides maximum shock in a small amount of time at a very high cost in material — fuel, bombs, etc. Main problem — lots of ads are TIVO'd out, and many viewers get up during commercials to go to the bathroom. Every year during Super Bowl commercials, water usage goes way, way up — that's the flush factor.

National advertisers use print media — consumer magazines and newspapers — like military warriors use the infantry. By using them, you can occupy and hold territory that has already been softened up by other media, such as TV (air force) and outdoor advertising (artillery). Once you've established your position, you can hold it with print at a relatively low cost. So national advertisers use print when their resources are rather limited.

Armored tanks are great for surprise attacks against established competition. Warner-Lambert used radio and only radio in a market-by-market campaign to reintroduce long-forgotten Corn Huskers Lotion and successfully position it as a workingman's hand lotion. Tanks and radio both work very well to outflank a strongly entrenched competitor.

Direct mail and targeted e-mails are airborne attacks. Why? Because they are the most demographically and geographically selective medium of all. But they're also the most expensive, cost-per-thousand-wise. Like a parachute, direct mail and targeted e-mails give you the pinpoint precision other media can't. They can also be camouflaged to keep your competitors in the dark — unless one of your competitors' marketing managers ends up on the mailing list you rent. Use them to gain control of smaller, isolated target markets.

How to Evaluate the Effectiveness of Your Promotion Campaign

What do you want your persuasive message aimed at your target audience to accomplish? You can't evaluate how effective your messages are unless you know in advance what it is you want them to do.

- Do you want your sales to increase?

- Do you want to change attitudes?

- Do you want to increase distribution?

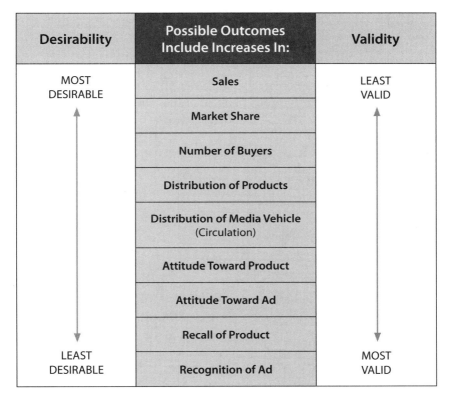

Desirability	Possible Outcomes Include Increases In:	Validity
MOST DESIRABLE	Sales	LEAST VALID
	Market Share	
	Number of Buyers	
	Distribution of Products	
	Distribution of Media Vehicle (Circulation)	
	Attitude Toward Product	
	Attitude Toward Ad	
	Recall of Product	
LEAST DESIRABLE	Recognition of Ad	MOST VALID

Measuring the value of an advertisement requires a tradeoff between the desirability of the outcome and the validity of the measure.

Figure 10.2. Nine outcomes of advertising

Figure 10.2 shows you nine possible outcomes of a marketing communications program, listed from most desirable to least desirable. It's nice to want to measure the sales effectiveness of your ads, but it's much easier to measure precisely the effectiveness of the outcomes at the bottom of the list than at the top, like recall of the ad. Marketers must make tradeoffs between desirability and measurement validity.

Recall of the ad itself is the most valid but the least desirable outcome of advertising. Here's what happens: Many consumer product advertisers use Starch Research's advertising measurement service (StarchResearch.com), which gives recognition scores of ads appearing in magazines — noted, read most, etc. However, advertisers often don't know what to do with those scores. They get back the Starch results, look at them, then put them in some file on their computer. They're soon forgotten. They take action only when scores are low. That's when they criticize or even fire their agencies. Sometimes, of course, they take action when scores are high — that's when they show the Starch Report to their bosses.

Sales are the least valid but most desirable outcomes. Many things can cause a sale — low price, great packaging, good shelf position, availability in all kinds of stores, advertising, etc. (see Figure 10.3). Even though a great advertising campaign may not be completely responsible for increased sales, ad agencies like to take credit for it. Business warfare is an art, not a science. So go ahead and have fun with it. And make a lot of money in the process. That's the mark of a winning warrior.

Advice on Holding Sales Contests

Below are six tips on how to reward your sales reps using sales contests:

1. Select prizes and awards that have value: Unusual things the sales reps would not get for themselves are bigger motivators. How can a rep get excited about a new shirt or blouse?

2. Don't forget the rep's spouse: The prize should appeal to the spouse. That way, you get help from the spouse in motivating the rep.

3. Get outside help to set up the contest: Many firms specialize in this. Find them online, ask your ad agency, trade association, etc.

4. Terms must be very clear: Make sure reps understand them completely. This leads to fewer arguments and problems later, and morale doesn't fall.

5. Interest must be kept high throughout the contest. How? Give periodic feedback, keep reminding reps of prizes to be won, etc.

6. Announce the winners: Do it dramatically. Always present the prizes in person, in front of all the reps.

How to Engage in Personal Selling — Be a Consultant, Not a Sales Rep

Too often, sales reps focus on what they can *get from* the buyer instead of what they can *do for* the buyer. The buyer can sense when the sales rep doesn't have the buyer's interests at heart. When this happens, a climate of mistrust develops, and it will be much harder to make a sale.

Advertising	Factors to Be Considered	Personal Selling
Many	Buyers — number	Few
Low	Cost of reaching prospects	High
Final customer	Customer — type	Distributor
Low	Effectiveness in creating sale	High
High	Efficiency in reaching prospect	Low
Low	Flexibility	High
High	Importance before sale	Low
Low	Importance during the sales pitch	High
High	Importance after sale	Low
Dispersed	Geographic concentration of buyers	Concentrated
Low	Price per unit sold	High
Standardized	Product — type	Complex
Delay — often long	Response	Immediate
Minimal	Service requirements	Considerable
Uncommon	Use of trade-ins	Common
High	Waste (poor prospect)	Medium

Figure 10.3. When to emphasize advertising or personal selling in your promotion mix

I tell sales reps in my seminars on salesmanship, negotiating, and how to influence others to start thinking like consultants instead of like sales reps. I even suggest they change their business cards to read Management Consultant or Marketing Consultant instead of Account Executive, Sales Representative, or Sales Engineer. At times, a consultant will have to say, "I don't think my product or service fits your needs this time. You'll be better off buying my competitor's product or service instead." A consultant would do this because the buyer's needs come first. The sales rep who acts like a consultant will lose a sale in the short run but gain more sales in the long run because the buyer knows the sales rep cares about the buyer.

Another way to gain the buyer's trust is to do your homework. Know as much about your buyer's marketing mix as the buyer does — or even more. Wow the buyer with your insights, knowledge, and wisdom. Show the buyer how your product or service can help solve the organization's marketing problems. Get the buyer to accept you as an industry marketing expert.

It's important to gain the buyer's trust first, because before you can even begin to sell, *you must earn the right to learn the buyer's needs!* This won't be easy because the buyer's needs are among their most important possessions. The buyer guards these needs and objectives because they contain the secrets to the organization's future. So you can't learn them quickly. And some you'll never learn, just as you'll never learn all the needs of the person closest to you, your spouse. How many times have you awakened at 3 a.m., gotten up to go to the bathroom, and returned to bed to find your sleeping spouse smiling broadly? You'll never know what that smile was about, will you? And you won't get the password, either, will you? If you can never learn all your spouse's needs, how can you expect to learn all about your buyer's needs?

How can you earn the right to learn your buyer's needs? It's not enough to ask probing questions or to listen closely — with your eyes, watching body language, as well as with your ears. Instead, accept the fact that it'll take a long time to gain the buyer's confidence. You can build up that confidence by getting out of the selling mode and into the consulting mode. Do your homework and learn how the buyer's company markets its products or services. Impress the buyer with this knowledge and by making sure they know you're putting their needs ahead of your need to make a sale.

How to Choose Your Ad Agency

Here are questions you need to think about in picking the right agency to handle your business:

1. What is the agency's character? Philosophy? Policies? Reserved or innovative? Conservative or daring? Does it emphasize copy or visuals? Is advertising an end in itself, or an integral part of the marketing mix? Does the agency seem to favor certain media? Is it known as a creative shop? Or simply a media buying outfit?

2. What is its average length of service to its clients? What has been its account turnover?

3. How long have its people been with it? This includes key management personnel as well as copywriters, account executives, and art directors. What's the depth of talent there? Examine the turnover, depth of experience, and the number of people on the second and third levels as well as at the top level.

4. How creative is it? Are its ads memorable? Do they sell? Is the agency solely concerned with producing ads, or do they want to produce other kinds of material that can strengthen your selling efforts?

5. Does it have experience with companies and products or services similar to yours? Does it handle any of your competitors? What kind of product and market knowledge does it have? Does it seem to specialize in one field, or is it versatile? Will it show you case studies? What has it done in the past for similar accounts? Make sure you contact these companies to see if they were satisfied with the agency's service.

6. What will it charge you? Are the charges commensurate with its services? Are you paying for services you don't need or that you could do yourself? Examine the agency's accounting practices in detail. Will you be getting any unexpected bills? Cost overruns? If so, how often and how big? Will the agency give you an estimate in writing for everything?

7. What's the agency's financial position? Is it profitable? Liquid? What's its Dun & Bradstreet rating? What's its standing with media and suppliers? Do all media recognize the agency? Or is it affiliated only with certain media?

8. How would an account of your size fit in with its other accounts?

9. What's the growth of the agency? Are its billings sound and consistent or fluctuating?

10. Where is it located? Is it convenient to your needs? Are there branch offices?

11. If you select this agency, who will be doing what, when, and how? Is the team that'll be working with you aggressive? Do they show leadership qualities? Or are they merely water-testers? Will their work or thinking be rigid or stylized? Or will they approach each problem with a fresh perspective? Is their experience and background essentially right for your company and its needs? Are they overly involved with the mechanics of their own particular specialties? Or do they seem interested in applying their talents to the sale of your products or services? What kind of answers will they give you? What kinds of questions will they ask? What kind of interest will they show? Will the answers, questions, and interest suggest not only their capability but the kinds of personalities you and your staff can work with efficiently and comfortably?

12. Make sure that the agency makes a presentation to you at *your* office, not *theirs*. This should include a statement of its philosophy, ads it has done in the past, the backgrounds of the principals, and a sales pitch about why it's the one agency best suited for your account. At the presentation, see if the chemistry is good.

13. Does it have sound research capabilities? This includes research in copy, motivation, product planning, packaging, and so on.

14. How responsive will it be to your needs? Will agency people be available for personal contact as often as you need? What will be the convenience and speed of contact for both regular and emergency purposes?

15. How big is the agency? Would you be better off with a larger or smaller one?

16. What other services does it offer? Merchandising? Sales promotion? Public relations? Production? Sales training? Development of dealers? Packaging? Displays? Marketing planning? What does it charge for each service?

Why Ad Agencies Get Fed Up and Drop Clients

Here's what ad agencies complain about the most — in other words, what you shouldn't do when working with your agency:

1. You have too many levels of approval.

2. You aren't willing to spend enough money to get the advertising job done the right way, the way they recommend.

3. You don't allow your agency to make a profit. You're not familiar with their cost constraints. You give them too many *make-work/keep 'em busy* projects.

4. You allow too many important decisions to be made by junior executives. There's not enough senior-level management involvement at times. There's too much personnel turnover, so the agency doesn't know who to talk to.

5. You don't follow established lines of communication. You don't communicate with your agency, not at the top, at the middle, or at the bottom. Top-level executives should communicate regularly to people at your agency to air major issues arising as part of day-to-day operations. This keeps junior-level executives from rocking the boat because they don't know any better.

6. You're afraid of experimenting, risk-taking, and innovating. You don't show initiative. The head of a leading ad agency once said, "Don't be afraid to try something new. Expect your agency to keep innovating. Don't expect your agency to be right every time, but be sure the chances for success are always good. Don't give up something that is good too soon. Don't ask for great ads — insist instead on great campaigns."

7. You aren't willing to listen to other points of view. You think you're always right.

8. You aren't open and honest with your agency.

9. You don't give enough lead time to your agency. There are too many emergencies because you don't plan ahead.

10. You hold too many unproductive and unnecessary meetings.

11. You rely too much on research and not enough on their judgment. You don't ask them the right questions.

12. You don't stick to schedules.

13. You don't make your agency feel secure. To overcome this problem, don't use the people there as scapegoats when sales fall. Liberate them from fear. The ad executive David Ogilvy once said, "Most agencies run scared, most of the time. Two reasons: Many of the people who gravitate to the agency business are naturally insecure. Many clients make it plain they are always on the lookout for a new agency. Frightened people are powerless to produce good advertising."

14. Quite often, you aren't willing to take a position. You vacillate too much. You fail to operate with your agreed-upon strategy or tactics. There's too much change for the sake of change. You aren't willing or able to set priorities.

Place Wars

How to Choose Your Distributors

Identifying and adding specific distributors is a regional or local decision — not done by people at the top, acting alone. Your regional sales managers should search for distributors in one or two key cities in the region. Use trade directories, phone books, and the internet. Get references from your contacts. Sometimes you can persuade your current distributor (or an employee who wants to move out on his or her own) to set up a branch office in the new area.

Once you have several potential distributors in mind, get together with your sales managers and pick the best candidate. Use the checklist below. And you can use the same checklist to evaluate the job they do.

1. What's the distributor's attitude toward the allowances and co-op promotional efforts you offer? Does it really want to handle your line? Or is it going after your line because of present shortages? Do you think you'll be dropped after the shortages ease?

2. Does it carry competitive products?

3. Does it cover the territory you want covered? Any overlap with any other distributors you use?

4. How many of the important prospects in its territory does it sell to? How many of them are missing from its customer list?

5. What is its on-time delivery record?

6. Does it have adequate business experience? What are its sales management, financial control, recordkeeping, warehousing, and inventory control practices like?

7. How well-established is it? Is it a one-person operation? If so, how experienced is the owner? What territory does it actually cover with its sales reps? Any plans for succession when the owner retires?

8. What is its physical plant like? Is there enough warehouse space, properly laid out, to enable it to carry adequate stocks of your line? Are there convenient sidings or truck approaches to its warehouse? Does it receive goods at convenient hours? Is there a back-up generator if you are selling refrigerated or frozen foods?

9. What are its service facilities like? Will it keep an adequate inventory for services?

10. Is it adequately financed? What is its financial position? This includes accounts receivable, cash position, debts, inventories, fixed assets, payment records, current ratio, acid-test ratio, total liabilities to net worth, and trends in these areas over the years. Does it pay its bills on time? Does it have the ability to discount its bills?

11. Does it have the ability to grow? Does it want to grow or does it like the status quo too much to even try?

12. Does it have adequate product knowledge, technical and otherwise? If not, can the distributor get it? Is the distributor willing to train its sales reps?

13. Is it willing to carry a full line of products to service all customer needs? Does it carry competing product lines? If so, will that cause a problem for your company? Or will those products add to the prestige of your products? Do these products complement or supplement yours and help facilitate your sales?

14. What is its market share or penetration in the area you're interested in?

15. Does it have the ability to get new business? How much has it gotten lately?

16. Will it be satisfied in some areas with less desirable outlets to avoid overlapping into the areas of your other distributors?

17. Are its price policies compatible with yours? Does it maintain stable prices? Does it initiate price wars?

18. What kind of trade contacts does it have? What kind of reputation and standing does it have with the trade — other manufacturers, distributors, and customers? How long has it been in business?

19. What's the quality of its sales force? How aggressive is it? How good are its sales reps? How many reps are there? How well-trained are they? Any objections to you helping out with training them?

20. What's its historical trend of sales volume, measured against the performance requirements established by your regional sales manager?

21. What's its annual inventory turnover? Will it tell you its annual sales figures for the last five years? If not, what is it hiding from you? Will it be easy or hard to find out?

22. What's the quality of its service to customers? Is it willing to perform after-the-sale service?

23. How many office employees does it have? Other indicators of size?

24. Is it willing to carry adequate stocks? Is that stock secure against theft and slippage (employee theft)?

Complaints About Distributors

Keep evaluating your distributors, especially after the honeymoon period is over. Here are the most common complaints manufacturers have against their distributors. If you have most of these complaints, it's probably time to get a new distributor.

1. They don't stress your brand name. You're just another product in a long list of products.

2. They can't or won't meet your territorial goals.

3. Their objectives are much different from yours.

4. They're very independent businesspeople — too independent!

5. They don't carry sufficient inventory levels to serve their customers rapidly.

6. They're lazy — they want all customers to come to them.

7. They don't follow your suggested pricing.

8. They primarily sell on price, not on the value of your product.

9. They aren't good at helping their customers solve problems they have with your products.

10. They don't emphasize your product lines enough.

11. They don't use your promotional materials.

12. They don't give you information about who their customers are and where they're located.

13. They have no succession plans, and some of the main people there are quite old.

14. They don't use your factory personnel or your sales territory managers effectively.

Why do these problems happen? The underlying reason is that distributors are entrepreneurs at heart, not bureaucratic, organization-oriented people like many line and staff executives are in producers' firms. (I hope you're entrepreneurial, not a bureaucrat.) If properly coached, the independent industrial distributor will work *with* you, but never work *for* you in a subordinate relationship. That hurts the ego of an executive in the producer's organization who is used to having people follow orders. Are you upset with your distributors because of your own ego problems or because they're incompetent? Be honest with yourself.

What Distributors Want to Know About Your Product

1. Will your new product cannibalize your old ones? Which products are more profitable: the cannibalized old ones or the new one?

2. How compatible is your new product with what they now carry?

3. Is the product guaranteed?

4. How much inventory will they have to carry?

5. Will you support the new product with enough national, local, regional, and cooperative advertising and promotion to keep it moving at a profitable rate?

6. What kinds of merchandising and promotional allowances will you give them? Will that be sufficient?

7. Does the new product fill an honest consumer need or want? And has this need been verified by consumer research?

8. Are there any shelf-stacking difficulties from the product package? Is it compatible with their warehouse's physical handling system? Is the packaging attractive?

9. How many competitive products are sold locally? How many other distributors are there in the same trading area? Is the new product established in terms of local user acceptance in other markets?

10. Is the new product better than one or more of those they now carry? What are the comparative values per pound? Sales potential?

11. What is the product's shelf life?

12. Will the new product add sufficient profit and volume to justify them carrying it?

13. Is your introductory promotional effort strong enough to get enough customers to try it? Is the introductory trade allowance high enough to cover start-up expenses?

14. Is the quota you give them realistic and challenging?

15. What is your reputation in terms of local user acceptance? In terms of the image of your company and brand name? This has to do both with final consumers and in past dealings with your distributors. Regarding past dealings:

    - What's your reputation for speed, consistency, and reliability in deliveries?

    - Do you have a clear, settled, consistent, printed policy in dealing with distributors?

    - What is your financial rating?

    - What is your factory capacity?

    - What is your access to raw materials?

    - What is your existing sales volume?

16. What will you do about slow-moving stock? Damaged goods?

17. Is the suggested selling price competitive?

18. Will you give them technical assistance? Do you conduct training programs? Offer other kinds of sales cooperation?

19. What happened to the product in test markets? How are other distributors doing with it?

Are You a Great Business Warrior?

Well, that was a lot of marketing info. How much of it was new to you? If a lot of it was new, you may be thinking:

- Should I go back to the university and re-take Marketing 101?

- Should I buy a lot of university textbooks on the subject?

- Should I buy a lot of trade books?

- Should I attend seminars and bring one or two good ideas back to work? My boss will give me a pat on the head, but will that advance my career?

You may not need to do any of these things. Maybe you're already a very good Business Warrior. Here's a way for you to find out how good — or how bad — you are. Do this in-basket case study.

Marketing Mix Variable	Autos	Auto Parts	Life Insurance	Plain White Bread
Product				
Distribution				
Price				
Advertising				
Personal selling				
Sales promotion				

Figure 10.4. The Business Warrior's worksheet

In-Basket Case Study: The Business Warrior's Worksheet

Figure 10.4 is a worksheet I use in my Business Warfare seminars. Executives who have used it have told me it's one of the simplest yet most valuable tools in their arsenals of weapons. This is how you can use it:

1. Assume you're the manufacturer, not a distributor.

2. Use a rating scale of 0 to 5. Assign *importance values* to each of the six marketing-mix variables. Automatically give a 5 to the most important variable for each of the four products. Work on one product at a time, though, not on all four at once. Rate the other five variables in relation to that most important one. You can give the same number to more than one marketing variable. A zero means you feel that particular marketing variable has absolutely no importance at all for that particular product.

3. Now put the numbers you think are best for automobiles (durable goods), automotive parts (component parts), life insurance (intangibles), and plain white bread (staples).

Marketing Mix Variable	Autos	Auto Parts	Life Insurance	Plain White Bread
Product	5	1	2	1
Distribution	2	5	4	5
Price	2	1	2	4
Advertising	3	1	3	2
Personal selling	1	3	5	1
Sales promotion	2	1	1	1

Figure 10.5. The Business Warrior's worksheet — filled out

4. When you've finished, look at Figure 10.5, which shows you how I allocated my numbers.

5. Read my reasoning. See if you agree with it or not.

After you've finished my numbering process and read my reasoning, you'll probably find that you and I have disagreed on some of the numbers we put into the worksheet. Agreeing or disagreeing with me isn't that important. What *is* important is the logical thought processes we both went through in deciding on our numbers.

So have the members of your brand group assign numbers to your brand independently. Then, at a group meeting, have everybody show their numbers to everybody else. Encourage a good argument. Should you try to get your reasoning and numbers accepted by everybody else? That's up to you. How big is your ego, anyway?

There won't be complete agreement. There never is. The hammering-out of your strategy and tactics at that meeting will be one of the most valuable experiences of your business life. I guarantee it! Why am I that positive? Because this is what many of the executives who have taken my seminars have told me.

Automobiles

The product, the car itself, is most important to most people, in my opinion, so I gave it a 5.

I gave a 2 to distribution because I don't think Ford will increase its market share substantially by adding a new dealer in a given town. (Most towns have enough dealers already.) Very few people will buy a Ford instead of a Chrysler because the Chrysler dealer is a few blocks closer.

Price got a 2 from me because I think the manufacturing costs of all automobile manufacturers are about the same for comparable models. Ford could outsell Chevrolet easily if it could price its cars 50 percent below Chevrolet's price, but Ford probably only has less than $50 to play around with because of comparable manufacturing costs. (If you considered this from the point-of-view of a retail car dealer, price would probably receive a 5.)

Advertising received a 3 because it's very important in establishing a desirable product image.

Personal selling is rated very low, with a 1, because the Ford sales rep who calls on the Ford dealer is not that important to creating sales. (Again, from the viewpoint of a retail car dealer, personal selling would probably receive a 4 or 5.)

I gave a 2 to sales promotion because manufacturers supply banners and displays to dealers and come up with contests that build showroom traffic.

Automotive Parts

I gave distribution a 5 because I think it's the *most* important variable. Why?

First, final consumers don't have much of a brand preference for spark plugs. They can't tell one spark plug from another, so product received only a 1. Most of the time they take their cars to a mechanic with a good reputation and rely upon his or her expertise to choose the right brand of parts for their cars.

Furthermore, parts usually make up a very small percentage of total repair bills in the United States, with the opposite occurring in underdeveloped nations. So price also received only a 1.

The back rooms of most garages are quite small, and there's only room for perhaps one brand of each part. Therefore, it's essential to get distribution of your parts with the best mechanics in the area. As a result, the parts sales rep who calls on the mechanics is very important in the marketing mix, so I gave personal selling a 3.

Advertising of auto parts is done on some sports programs on TV, mainly for the mechanic to see. The mechanic would rather carry a known brand, rather than an unknown one. Therefore, I decided to give advertising a 1.

Finally, sales promotion is usually limited to the calendars that the mechanic hangs up in the back room. This isn't too important, so I only gave it a 1.

Life Insurance

Intangibles need to be pointed out, explained, and demonstrated, so personal selling is the most important variable and rates a 5.

Getting the right agent to handle your brand of insurance is very important, because people who buy insurance do so mainly because they have confidence in the agent. Therefore, distribution is given a 4.

Agents like to handle policies of companies that are well known, so advertising rates a 3.

Most insurance policies are similar, and most people don't even read them. Therefore, product only rates a 2.

It's hard to use price competition in insurance because of the intangible nature of the product, so I gave it a 2 as well.

Finally, people don't change agents because they like one calendar better than another, so sales promotion only gets a 1.

Plain White Bread

People won't make a special effort to go to another store to buy a different brand of bread. Instead, they'll choose from the brands offered in the store they usually shop in. Therefore, distribution is extremely important, and I gave it a 5.

Because bread is a staple and purchased often, consumers know that even small price differences *add up* over a period of time. Therefore, price is quite important, and I felt it deserved a rating of 4.

The only reason I gave a 2 to advertising is that sometimes children will demand a particular brand they see on TV. Advertising isn't that important to the adult bread market, though.

Neither is product, which received a 1, because plain white bread is a very homogeneous product with very little opportunity for product differentiation. The only way you can differentiate it is by freshness, and this quality varies over time.

Bread sales reps are probably misnamed: They usually just deliver, not sell. They are usually hired for their strong backs, not for their strong minds. Therefore, personal selling rates only a 1.

Finally, sales promotion also deserves a 1 because it's seldom used. But occasionally a bread manufacturer will supply special display stands, banners, and so on to a store for goodwill purposes.

Moving Forward: Your Plan of Action

If you just skimmed the book, you missed a lot of good stuff. Use it as a handbook. Keep it close to you. Pick it up from time to time. Read more and more. Take notes. Eventually you'll become an even better Business Warrior than you are now.

365 Winning Weapons

I want to leave you with a gift — the 365 winning weapons I developed over the years to get people to do what you want them to do.

Participants in my two-day seminar, *How You Can Negotiate and Win*, master the 365 weapons-techniques you'll read about in this chapter. I've given the seminar in 36 nations on 6 continents to over 50 nationalities. Toward the end of my seminar, I ask them what tactics they use the most in 11 different situations — 5 business, 5 personal, and dealing with a hostile attorney. (The last situation could be either personal or business). Figure 11.1 shows the results from 12 nations — contrasting Americans' favorite weapons with favorite weapons used by 11 other nationalities.

You'll notice I left the last deal-making situation blank. Why? Because sexual favors is the only situation where almost everybody in those 36 nations — including Americans — agreed. But it's also the only situation where men were very different from women. Men really liked to use *smooth talk, flattery,* and *charm* (Assertive Weapon #60), whereas women loved to use *make men aware of their competition — real or imaginary* (Defensive Weapon #4). That's because, almost everywhere, men are the pursuers and women are the pursued.

Executives from the United States	Deal-Making Situation	Executives from Other Nations
Size matters — the big pot (Assertive 48)	**Seller: Get the buyer to pay more**	*Chile:* Threaten dooms-day (Assertive 112)
Say "Take it or leave it" and be prepared to walk away — Elvis has left the building (Assertive 68)	**Buyer: Get the seller to lower the price**	*Great Britain* and *Australia:* Remind the other side of their competition — real or imaginary (Defensive 4)
Let's look at the record (Assertive 104)	**Ask your boss for a raise**	*Brazil:* Find allies and use them (Defensive 76)
Let's look at the record (Assertive 104)	**Ask your boss for a promotion**	*New Zealand:* Go way beyond what you have to do (Cooperative 21)
Anticipate objections and defuse them in advance (Defensive 13)	**Change your vacation at the last minute**	*Thailand:* Make prom-ises instead of conced-ing (Cooperative 13)
Control the agenda (Assertive 53)	**Deal with a hostile attorney**	*Indonesia:* The power of powerlessness and creeping paralysis (Defensive 1)
Size matters — the big pot (Assertive 48)	**Buy a house**	*Philippines:* Remind the other side of their competition — real or imaginary (Defensive 4)
Size matters — the big pot (Assertive 48)	**Sell your car**	*Malaysia:* Say "Take it or leave it" and be prepared to walk away — Elvis has left the building (Assertive 68)

Figure 11.1. Tactics favored by executives in 11 deal-making situations

Executives from the United States	Deal-Making Situation	Executives from Other Nations
Admit your mistakes and apologize before you're blamed (Defensive 85)	**Get out of a traffic ticket**	*Kenya:* Bribe them (Dirty Trick 20)
Momentum: Always keep pressure on them (Assertive 66)	**Get your children to pick up their clothes**	*Hong Kong:* Make the other side feel guilty (Assertive 80)
	Sexual favors — from a friend (not a prostitute)	

Figure 11.1 (continued). Deal-making tactics favored by executives

 WEB ALERT

If you would like to have specific details of favorite tactical weapons used in 11 situations by people in 36 different nations, by men versus women, by Big Dogs versus Guerrillas, etc., please go to GuerrillaDon.com for details.

The winning weapons are broken into six groups:

- Preparation weapons
- Assertive weapons
- Defensive weapons
- Submissive weapons
- Cooperative weapons
- Dirty tricks

The 100 most powerful weapons are *italicized*. I've also noted the fifty most *under*-used and 50 most *over*-used weapons.

You can read more about the fifty under-used and fifty over-used weapons in great detail in two of my books, *365 Powerful Ways to Influence* and *Guerrilla Deal-Making*. *Guerrilla Deal-Making* also gives you 400 winning counter-punches to the 100 most powerful weapons.

Preparation Weapons

Begin preparing

1. Think ahead. Circumstances are always changing.

2. Pick your battles carefully. Prepare, rehearse, manage your time.

3. Avoid paralysis of perfectionism. Set priorities. Use the 80-20 rule.

4. *Think on your feet — learn from children. Overcome paralysis of not thinking fast enough — children are creative, uninhibited. (Under-used)*

5. *You've got to earn the right to learn TOS's needs. Gain their confidence. Become comfortable with ambiguity. (Under-used)*

6. Have empathy. Put yourself in TOS's place.

7. Be skeptical. Become hard to convince.

> ## The Other Side: TOS
>
> Throughout this chapter I use the acronym TOS for the other side — your enemy, your competition, or maybe just the person sitting across the table from you during negotiations.

Control your ego

8. *Don't give away the store to see TOS smile. It's OK to let TOS dislike you. (Under-used)*

9. Understand the power of blind spots. Know yours and TOS's.

10. Your ego — lose it. Deal with your ego — concentrate on winning the negotiation.

11. *Admit your mistakes, learn from them. Be honest with TOS and with yourself. (Under-used)*

Leave your tensions and negative emotions behind

12. Calm down and lighten up. Relax yes, tense no.

13. *Escalation is stupid. Don't throw good money after bad. (Under-used)*

Be daring

14. Dare to fail. Fear of failure — lose it.

15. Be spontaneous. Prepare well and trust your instincts.

16. *Thinking small is smart. When you have less to lose, you feel you can do anything. It's a big advantage over Big Dogs who have more to lose and are more cautious. (Under-used)*

Demonstrate commitment and integrity

17. Commit totally. Highly committed means highly focused. Together they mean a big winner — you!

18. Show integrity. Never compromise your basic objectives.

Make concessions

19. *Learn the fine art of concession-making. There are twenty dos and twenty don'ts. Learn them and use them.[1] (Over-used)*

Pay attention to order

20. Discuss easiest issues first — you'll get momentum that way.

21. Use a one-minute sales pitch (elevator speech) on strangers making your strongest offerings.

22. Get momentum by making the first offer (I'll show you mine, then you show me yours).

23. *Get TOS to make the first offer — get powerful knowledge that way (Show me yours, then I'll show you mine). (Over-used)*

Apply finishing touches

24. Don't be too satisfied when it's over — stay a little hungry. If you're completely satisfied, you won too much and TOS will be unhappy.

25. Be in good physical condition. Enough sleep plus moderate eating and drinking equals less stress.

26. *Negotiate on an empty stomach. Physical hunger leads to psychological hunger. When you want more, you'll get more (Under-used)*

27. *Mornings are good, afternoons not so much. The best deal-making time is 10:30 a.m. The worst is 2:30 p.m. (Under-used)*

---

1. You can find 20 dos and don'ts of concession-making in my book *Guerrilla Deal-Making*, Chapter 17.

28. Be curious, not sad, about TOS's objections. Find out why they object and do something about it.

29. Be passionate and enthusiastic about your cause. Passion and enthusiasm soon become contagious.

Become a master strategist

30. Learn and master chess. It's a great way to learn strategy. Use the techniques you learn in persuading TOS.

31. When you do things right, TOS won't be sure you did anything at all. Use a light touch, lose your ego, win more.

Assertive Weapons

Distraction Weapons

Try the basic weapon

1. *Make sudden, unexpected moves. Distract TOS, put them off-balance. They won't expect your next move. (Under-used)*

Take advantage of surprise

2. Attack TOS's ego. Abuse them with sarcasm.

3. Surprise TOS — bring an expert. Especially if they're from out-of-town.

4. Surprise TOS — give them new information. Please them with new data important to them.

5. Surprise TOS with new issues, broader problems. Have a change of heart or insist on new rules.

6. Use bipolar negotiating tactics — exhibit very abrupt mood swings.

7. Unexpectedly change team leaders or have no team leader.

8. Make strange changes in your team's makeup. For example, on day one your team comprises all big, tough-looking men; on day two all very short women.

9. Surprise with frequent time changes — meeting times, deadlines, etc.

10. Surprise with frequent location changes — meeting rooms, addresses, even cities.

Pretend

11. *Play dumb to be smart. Say "Who me? Sorry, I didn't know."*
     (Over-used)

12. Pretend you don't know the local language. Eavesdrop to get
     valuable information.

13. Pretend you don't know the local customs. "Get away with
     murder" that way.

14. Pretend you believe TOS (even though you know they're
     lying), put them off balance, and then zap them at the end.

15. *Act astonished! Pretend you can't believe what TOS is telling you.*
     Say "Aieeee!" (Over-used)

16. Show pain when you concede, using both face and voice.

Use other distractions

17. *Turn your liabilities into assets. First impressions are wrong, but*
     lasting. Disarm TOS, and then zap them at the end. (Under-used)

18. *Be wild and crazy. Put on a good show by acting that way.*
     (Under-used)

19. *Don't give TOS your best offer too soon. Laying all your cards on*
     the table too soon is stupid. (Over-used)

20. *For sellers — make buyers pursue you for a change. Say "Why*
     should I deal with you instead of your competitor?" (Under-used)

21. When TOS is angry, distract them. Raise another issue to
     distract them from their anger instead of groveling.

22. Flirt — attract, reject, then attract again. Become pursued. This
     often works better for women than men.

Moderately Assertive Weapons

Capitalize on time

23. Know when to speak, when to pause. Respond slowly when
     it's in your best interest. The know-when is as important as the
     how-to.

24. *Don't accept TOS's first offer too quickly. Avoid buyer's remorse.*
     Eager beavers are losers. (Over-used)

25. *Use the rule of three — a Chinese favorite. Say no at least three times before finally saying yes. (Under-used)*

26. Stretch out the negotiation over a long period of time.

27. *Make TOS invest a lot of their time (the car dealer's delight). (Under-used)*

28. *Set wise and shrewd deadlines. In negotiations, 80 percent of the action takes place in the 20 percent of time just before the deadline. TOS's deadline is their problem, not yours. (Over-used)*

Profit by knowledge

29. Be suspicious — look for and penetrate TOS's three Ss — learn their shields, smokescreens, and scams.

30. Take advantage of TOS's three Ss — use their shields, smokescreens, and scams against them.

31. *Take advantage of TOS's blind spots. Find them — it's easier than you think. (Over-used)*

32. *Know your enemy and know yourself. Knowledge is power, said Sun Tzu in* The Art of War. *(Under-used)*

33. Be logical. And make sure TOS knows that you are.

Involve other people

34. Use gatekeepers — yours and TOS's. You can control access this way.

35. *Divide and conquer. Concentrate on the person on TOS's team mostly likely to say yes. Win him or her over to help you. (Over-used)*

36. *Turn TOS's top assistants into heroes. They'll be grateful and help you. (Under-used)*

37. Use professionals or agents to negotiate for you. If you're inexperienced, get help.

Brag (or not)

38. *Act arrogant. Overwhelm TOS — pull rank. (Over-used)*

39. *Act egotistical. Convince TOS that you're the greatest! (Over-used)*

40. Take advantage of the bandwagon effect — lead a parade. Tell TOS about your many satisfied customers.

41. *Imply your power — don't intentionally display it. Be subtle — use body language, smell good, be clean, carry very little. (Under-used)*

42. Dress very well. Read *Dress for Success* books, fashion magazines.

43. Dress sloppily on purpose so TOS will underestimate you.

Consider transparent weapons

44. *Use good guy, bad guy tactics. Negotiate as a two-person team. (Over-used)*

45. *Scare, then rescue, TOS. Realistically predict terrible future events if they don't solve their problems. Tell them you can solve their problems. (Under-used)*

46. Make TOS depend on you. It's easier to manipulate them this way. For example, "golden handcuffs" retirement plans.

47. *Use a decoy. Pretend you want X. Give it up to get Y, which is what you really want. (Over-used)*

48. *Use the Big Pot. Ask for a lot more than you expect to get. (Over-used)*

49. Use the Little Pot. Always start with a low bid at auctions.

50. *Bluff — it's the not-too-obvious lie. It's always expected. TOS gets suspicious if you don't bluff. (Over-used)*

Weapons to Confront, Control, and Overwhelm

Confront

51. Confront TOS — call their bluff. Say "Prove to me you mean what you say."

52. Confront TOS when they use dirty tricks. Say "Why are you using dirty tricks? When will you stop?"

Control

53. Control the agenda. Set formal rules. Don't let TOS bring up anything else without your consent.

54. Control the agreement process. Write down every agreement in your own words. Both TOS and you will initial it.

55. Limit what your team can tell TOS. Make sure TOS's team learns only what you want them to know.

Overwhelm

56. *Use your wish list to overwhelm TOS. Most reality lists contain four items maximum. (Over-used)*

57. Negotiate at your place. You have more power there.

58. *Engage in Tuangou, swarming ambushes, flash mobs. Social media bring many people together. Meet at the store. Demand large discounts for everyone on big-ticket items. (Under-used)*

59. Overwhelm TOS with lots more people on your team.

White Lies, Borderline Aggression, and The Power of No Weapons

Exploit your white lies

60. *Use smooth talk, charm, flattery. Say "My deal is for smart people only, and you're obviously smart." (Over-used)*

61. *Show off your knowledge. Convince TOS you have lots of information, even if you don't. (Over-used)*

62. Exaggerate slightly, but not too much. It's expected on both sides.

Apply borderline aggression

63. Get paid first, then perform. You'll keep all the power that way. The value of your service declines dramatically after you perform it.

64. *Take it first, then talk about it. Act first, reach your goal, then see what TOS does about it. Don't apologize — this reduces your power. (Under-used)*

65. Never pay in advance. You'll keep your power that way. Watch out for scams.

66. *Always keep pressure on TOS. Get momentum at the very beginning. (Over-used)*

67. Deliver a powerful ultimatum. Convince TOS you'll do anything to win. They'll fear your unpredictability.

68. *Tell them "Take it or leave it" (Elvis has left the building). Leave if they say "No." (Over-used)*

69. Make TOS realize you're very committed to your goals. Stick to your plan no matter what.

70. Be brave, not scared. Don't let TOS intimidate you. Ignore their threats.

Rely on the power of no

71. Be stubborn — say "No." Offer no excuse. If you say "No" often enough, TOS will believe you. Be consistent.

72. *Never accept a "No" from TOS. They may be just testing you. Give them more reasons to say "Yes." (Over-used)*

Just Plain Mean and Nasty Weapons

Threaten

73. *Tell TOS "I'm getting ready to withdraw." Start to walk away to test their reaction. (Over-used)*

74. Tell TOS "I'm going over your head." Threaten to talk to their boss.

75. Tell TOS "I'm telling the news media." Public knowledge will put pressure on them.

76. Tell TOS "I'm telling government officials." Tell regulatory agencies, police, etc., if they're doing something illegal.

77. Threaten TOS with actual physical violence. The threat of violence is usually more powerful than actual violence. (Don't commit crimes.)

Engage in obvious intimidation

78. *Rely on tradition, custom, conformity. Intimidate TOS by saying "That's just the way we do things here." (Over-used)*

79. Take advantage of superstitions, slogans, proverbs. Google these words. Pick those that will intimidate TOS the most.

80. *Make TOS feel guilty. Put them on a guilt trip. (Over-used)*

81. Slander TOS. Make malicious statements about them. But remember that false statements can lead to lawsuits. (Don't commit crimes.)

82. Consider name-calling, stereotyping. But watch out! Insults can become self-fulfilling prophecies.

83. Stress your height — if you're taller. Intimidate TOS if you're very tall.

84. Leverage with money — the fact that you have more than TOS has. Gamblers will raise the pot to a level TOS can't match.

85. Act like Santa Claus. Make TOS think you can afford to give it away.

86. Make the most of lawful, legitimate power. Policemen have it. Having right on your side does not automatically give your this power, however.

87. Employ your charisma. Your winning personality can help you win.

88. *Reward or punish TOS. Bosses have this power. (Over-used)*

89. Use big words. A large vocabulary works only if you know your audience.

Use envy

90. Flaunt your title and status in the company. Line is superior to staff. People who don't delegate over-use this.

91. Flaunt your credentials — your degrees, honors, reputation.

92. Flaunt your prestigious occupation. Be careful. Firemen are more prestigious than architects. Check annual Harris polls.

93. *Become untouchable — intimidate TOS. Examples of potential untouchables include company owners, long-time employees, those sleeping with the boss, very good-looking people. (Under-used)*

94. Flaunt your expertise. Or bring a well-known expert from out-of-town with you if you're not an expert.

95. Flaunt your celebrity power. Celebrities are used to getting their way, but being spoiled turns off TOS — and celebrities attract con men.

Engage in subtle intimidation

96. Communicate indirectly — only through third parties (secretary, attorney, etc.).

97. *Put TOS on the defensive. Accuse them, make negative statements. Use this for brief periods only. (Over-used)*

98. Make stupid mistakes on purpose to put TOS off-balance. Use this rarely or TOS will think you're really dumb.

99. Make it easy for TOS to make stupid mistakes. Take advantage of them.

100. *Ignore TOS — have a deaf ear. Don't pay attention to what they say. Keep doing things your way. (Under-used)*

101. Pretend to lose your temper. Be a good actor. Use this sparingly.

Rely on endurance

102. Be flexibly persistent. Come up with major new and different ways to get what you want. Try them out, one after the other.

103. *Nibble away. Wear out TOS, outlast them. Get many minor things over time — they probably won't notice. (Over-used)*

104. *Look at the record. Use relevant facts, figures that show TOS how they'll benefit from your service. (Over-used)*

Put your foot in the door

105. Put your foot in door, barely. Propose a small initial order.

106. Put your foot in door, wiggle your toes. Keep asking for more and more small orders.

107. Put your foot in door, kick it in. Make a full-scale proposal.

Play games

108. Think and become more like a child. Learn how kids manipulate parents — use their tricks.

109. Consider rock, paper, scissors. When all else fails, break a deadlock with this children's game. Try others, too.

110. Cry on purpose — sympathy-seeking to the extreme.

111. Engage in dares, double dares, and the game of chicken. If TOS doesn't take the dare, they lose face.

112. Threaten doomsday. Predict disaster if TOS doesn't accept your offer.

Other Assertive Weapons

113. Remove your cellphone, watch. Make sure TOS notices that you're giving them your full attention.

114. Use rituals, symbols to formalize the agreement. For example, put the contract in an expensive leather binder.

115. Have the contract all ready to sign. Control things by preparing it ahead of time. Give it to TOS at the right time.

116. Be a rebel — buck the trend. Be unpredictable. Do the exact opposite, ignore conventional wisdom.

117. Never waste a crisis. TOS's catastrophe is your opportunity.

118. *Redirect ownership of the problem. Turn your problem into a joint problem, then into TOS's problem. (Over-used)*

119. Say "What if…?" and hope TOS says "How?" Launch a trial balloon and wait for their magic buying signal.

120. Challenge TOS in order to inspire them. Give TOS an important role. Use management by objectives (MBO).

121. Be sure — use off-setting bets. Don't put all your eggs in one basket.

Defensive Weapons

Power, Mind Games, Silence, Focus, Body Language, Concessions

Try subtle power

1. *Use the power of powerlessness and creeping paralysis. Say "Help me understand your position — that's the only way I can help you." Pretend you don't know how to use a photocopier so TOS will assist you each time. (Over-used)*

2. Ask for sympathy. Say "I'd like to do this for you, but my people won't back me up." Don't say "Poor me!"

3. Use TOS's sense of ethics, justice, morality. Make them think they're evil if they don't give in to you, the good guy.

4. *Remind TOS of their competition — real or imaginary. Remember, "You Doing Without" is their big competitor. (Over-used)*

Play mind games

    5. *Distract TOS — put them off-balance, Japanese-style. Take advantage of their rhythm when they're unsettled. Read Miyamoto Musashi's* Go Rin No Sho. *(Under-used)*

    6. *Use funny money, not real money. Use percentages (funny), not dollars (real). Percentages sound smaller. (Over-used)*

    7. Distract TOS with a minor skirmish elsewhere. For example, start a price war in a small, isolated area.

    8. Become an ostrich. Deny the problem exists.

    9. *Be apathetic, indifferent. Remember, the person with the* least *commitment to the relationship has the* most *power. (Under-used)*

Employ silence

    10. *Use complete, total silence. It's the best way to deal with TOS's lousy offer. (Under-used)*

    11. Don't react visibly to TOS's lousy offer. Don't let your facial expression give you away.

    12. Use the pregnant pause. Keep silent after your request. Wait for TOS to agree.

Focus on TOS

    13. Anticipate, minimize TOS's objections. State their objections before they can. Make them think the objections have no merit.

    14. *Lower TOS's expectations, keep them low. Don't raise them by conceding too fast, too often. (Over-used)*

Understand the value of body language
(the most important skill of influence)

    15. *Watch TOS's body language closely. Read my books, including* 365 Powerful Ways to Influence, *Chapter 11, and* Guerrilla Deal-Making, *Chapter 16. Practice what you've learned. (Under-used)*

    16. *Manipulate TOS with* your *body language. Read books, practice what you've learned. (Under-used)*

17. Employ reassuring body language. Read body language sections in books on flirting, and practice what you've learned.

18. *Apply touch power. Use the body language of touching. (Under-used)*

19. *Take advantage of position power. Set up your office to give you an advantage over TOS. (Under-used)*

Note concessions

20. *Notice concession patterns. Observe and record — both yours and TOS's.[2] (Under-used)*

Information Weapons

Get information

21. Appear harmless, then zap TOS at the end. Think *Columbo,* TV's bumbling detective.

22. Get and verify information — detect and expose bullshit. Research TOS and their company to see if they're lying.

Use information

23. Use assumptions wisely — both yours and TOS's. Change yours when necessary. Say early, "And how would you like to pay for this?"

Give information away

24. *Spread grapevine gossip. Leaking information through others is often more powerful than a direct message. (Under-used)*

Protect your information

25. Secure your secrets. Adopt a fortress mentality. Watch out for Internet hackers.

26. Hire a professional security firm. Don't be a cheap amateur.

---

2. You can find 20 dos and don'ts of concession-making in my book *Guerrilla Deal-Making,* Chapter 17.

Delaying Weapons

Engage in obvious delays

27. Stall for time. Have a big list of excuses.

28. Procrastinate openly. Show your discomfort in being rushed.

29. *Use the power of being unprepared. Forget on purpose. For example, forget your credit card, checkbook, etc. (Over-used)*

30. *Give TOS the run-around. Avoid seeing them, talking to them. Ignore their e-mails. (Over-used)*

31. Be very bureaucratic. Say "I have to follow the rules."

Say your well is dry

32. *You can't afford it. Say "I have no more money." (Over-used)*

33. You won't break the law. Say "I don't want to get in trouble."

34. Your hands are tied — your company won't let you. Prove it — talk about rules, regulations, precedents.

35. You won't go against your ethics. Say "I've got to follow my conscience."

Spin wheels — make TOS start all over again

36. Introduce new specifications. Delay by changing specifications slightly.

37. Make a new formal proposal. Delay by starting all over from scratch.

38. Come up with a surprise alternative. Delay by giving TOS something new to think about.

39. Add new issues to written agendas. Delay by bringing up new issues indirectly related to agenda.

Cloud, confuse, and complicate

40. Force information overload. Delay by giving TOS too much unimportant information, full of minor details.

41. Keep asking for more and more information. Delay things, but have good reason for asking.

42. *Don't give TOS very important information. Delay and learn how powerful you are by seeing how often TOS asks you for it. (Over-used)*

43. Explain an unimportant matter in great detail. Delay by pretending TOS really wants this information.

44. Insist on reading complicated stuff out loud. Delay things this way, but don't be obvious about it.

45. Keep talking so TOS can't talk. Delay by using the filibuster.

46. Make an extremely complicated change. Delay by setting up a different organizational structure, real or phony.

Consider transparent smokescreens

47. *Delay by saying, "My computer crashed. Lost lots of data. Have to redo it from memory" (My dog ate my homework). (Under-used)*

48. Delay by saying "My expert can't be here" (My dog ate my expert).

49. *Be honest — but only up to the point where it doesn't hurt you. Be cautious about laying your cards on the table before TOS does. (Over-used)*

50. Suddenly have to go to the toilet. Delay things this way.

51. Suddenly get very hungry, thirsty. Delay things this way.

52. Give a very poor explanation on purpose. Delay by using an inarticulate, inept spokesperson.

53. Use creative vagueness. Say things open to many interpretations. Let TOS fill in gaps themselves.

54. Change locations — occasionally, but not often. Delay by moving to less convenient locations.

55. Replace your team's leader, who will delay things by changing the rules.

56. Add team members who can slow things down. For example, legal staff, translators.

57. Use a silent buzzer — spontaneous interruptions. Delay by using the under-desk buzzer to get your secretary to interrupt the meeting.

58. *Lighten up — get off the subject for a while. Use humor, sports, small talk. (Under-used)*

Create black holes

59. Start many investigations, one after the other. Delay things this way.

60. Set up a fact-finding committee. Delay things this way.

61. Set up a study group. Delay things this way.

62. Set up a summit meeting. Delay things this way.

Miscellaneous Defensive Weapons

Use shields

63. Ignore realities. Concentrate on unrealistic possibilities instead. Be overly optimistic.

64. Avoid change by ignoring new information. Deny things can change.

65. Rationalize. When you can't get what you want, tell yourself "I didn't want it anyway."

66. Over-identify with your company. Your self-esteem comes from your job. You'll do everything you can to keep it.

67. Take an ego trip. Impress TOS by acting like a VIP.

68. Get compensation when you're dissatisfied. Don't be afraid to complain to the right people.

69. Exhibit subtle mood changes. Fluctuate between cheerfulness and mild anger.

70. Project your faults onto TOS. Dump on them, make them the scapegoat for your bad luck.

71. *Nag constantly — use low-level negativity. Nibble away by nagging away. Subtly bully people you think are weak. (Over-used)*

72. Make a strong attempt to dominate TOS. Make them cater to all your whims.

73. Act obnoxious and hostile. Try to intimidate TOS this way.

Use other people

74. Use a team, don't be the Lone Ranger. Build team spirit — make your team unified, friendly, competent. Give them respect, appreciation.

75. Join with others. For example, engage in management lock-
    outs, union strikes.

76. *Find allies and use them. Get others to help you, directly and
    indirectly, inside and outside of your company. (Under-used)*

77. Find prestigious allies and use them. TOS's ego will make them
    accept your offer, even when it's not as much as they want.

78. Reposition TOS. Make them not just your ally — make them
    your mentor.

Use news media

79. Get good publicity from news media. Make sure TOS hears
    about it.

80. Get bad publicity from news media. Playing the villain may
    make TOS fear you so much they give in.

81. Demonize somebody just for the publicity — not TOS, of
    course. Character assassination gives you publicity.

Act quickly when TOS catches you doing something naughty

82. Find a scapegoat. Blame your assistant when the deal goes
    wrong. Fire him or her. Make sure TOS knows you did this.

83. Say "Don't blame me, I didn't do it." Don't admit you made
    the mistake.

84. Say "Yes, I did it, but the devil made me do it." Blame somebody
    else for forcing you to make the mistake.

85. Admit your mistakes and apologize. Do this before TOS tries to
    blame you.

Defensive Weapons That Are Almost Assertive

86. Draw the worst-case scenario. Tactfully tell TOS all the bad
    things that could happen if you do what they want. Prepare
    them for all eventualities.

87. *Tell TOS "You gotta do better than that!" Tell them why you can't
    accept their offer. Tell them what's in it for them if they give you a
    better deal. Over-used)*

88. *Use trade-offs, but don't mess with promises. Give up your intangible X to get TOS's tangible Y. Intangible promises are easy to make, hard to keep. (Over-used)*

89. Don't give in to unreasonable demands. Keep your self-respect, don't lose your momentum.

90. Don't debate, counterattack instead. Keep some issues in reserve to use when TOS is too aggressive. Debate result — one wins, one loses. Negotiation result — both can win.

91. Make TOS pick the alternative you want. None of the alternatives should favor TOS — they all should favor you.

92. Make sure TOS has only one way out of danger — pleasing you. Make sure they know this is their only option.

Submissive Weapons

Concede on both sides

1. Put a dollar value on each concession both you and TOS make. Know how much you're conceding — ask your accountant.

Use time wisely

2. Buy time — promise TOS something. Make specific promises, not vague ones.

3. *Drool and choose. Give TOS a free trial on several attractive items. Ask them to buy the one they like best. (Over-used)*

Play word games

4. Say "Yes, but" — less powerful than *and*. Offer TOS a tentative agreement first, and then state your case under pleasant conditions. *But* is negative. *And* is positive.

5. Say "Yes, and" — more powerful than *but*. Offer TOS a tentative agreement first, and then state your case under pleasant conditions. *And* is positive. *But* is negative.

Exercise extreme submission

6. Don't argue — turn the other cheek instead. Let TOS get it off their chest. Don't confront them.

7. Be a sponge, not a wall. Make an inconsequential remark (sponge) when TOS tries to provoke you. A provocative answer (wall) makes things worse. Think about it: a ball bounces off a wall, not off a sponge.

8. Don't stand out — the nail that stands out gets hammered down. Avoid trouble — don't rock the boat.

9. Beg — and if that doesn't work, pray. Don't worry about losing face.

Give in and save face at the same time

10. Take one step at a time. Retreat to your previously prepared position and try again.

11. Make a contingent offer. Say "I'll do this if you do that."

12. Use the tough give-in. Bargain harder each time you give up something.

Get help

13. Go to your last resort. Use arbitration, mediation.

Engage in submission by stupidity

14. *Split the difference. Tempt TOS by making this offer. Whoever makes the offer first has the least to lose. (Over-used)*

15. Threaten self-destruction — "see me, catch me, stop me, save me." Appeal to TOS's sense of humanity.

Engage in submission by smarts

16. Take whatever you can get. If your time is worth more to you than TOS's time is worth to them, stop trying. Accept their offer and leave with your self-respect. (Over-used)

Cooperative Weapons

Apply the three essentials of cooperation

1. *Use the power of patience. Don't hurry — if you can afford to outwait TOS and they can't afford to outwait you, you'll win big. (Under-used)*

2. Make TOS happy. They'll become contented, and committed to you.

3. Be a consultant, not a sales rep. Concentrate on TOS's needs (consultant), not on your need to sell (sales rep).

Form an alliance with TOS

4. *Reciprocate. Say "If you scratch my back, I'll scratch yours." But don't create obligations neither side wants. (Over-used)*

5. Get the best ally of all — TOS themselves. Ask them "What would you do if you were me?" Brainstorm together.

6. Be intimate, without sex. Develop a close friendship, bonding with TOS.

7. Be intimate, with sex. It happens often. People have 237 reasons to have sex. Google it. Find your favorite reason.

Be honest

8. Be completely honest — reveal your bottom line. Impress TOS by laying all your cards on the table.

9. Tell TOS your shortcomings. Don't hide them when honesty gives you an advantage.

10. *Admit you don't know something. Don't hide it — you'll look even dumber if TOS catches you. Tell them when you'll get the information. (Under-used)*

Speak

11. Speak clearly so TOS won't misunderstand you.

12. Make it easy for TOS to say "Yes" early and often. Ask questions that most people will answer with a "Yes."

13. *Make tempting promises instead of conceding. Promise things important to TOS that you can actually do. Don't promise just to buy time. (Over-used)*

Listen

14. *Listen well — your cheapest and most important concession. Knowledge gives you power. Listening flatters TOS. Not listening insults them. (Under-used)*

15. *Listen actively. Use TOS's own words to emphasize the points you both agree upon. Google this for lots more information. (Under-used)*

Keep cooperating, even after the negotiation is over

16. *Give a bonus — something nice and unexpected. Tell TOS "Thanks" — give them something extra after the deal has been completed. (Under-used)*

17. When you win big, make sure TOS saves face. If you don't, they may back out or sabotage the deal.

18. *Make sure TOS looks good at the end. Show them how the agreement will help them in the eyes of their boss. (Under-used)*

19. *Make TOS think you lost, even if you won big. If they think you won too much, they may try to back out of the deal. Remember how the movie, The Sting, ended. (Under-used)*

Apply five degrees of cooperation

20. *Use mental seduction. Become indispensable by over-cooperating. Make TOS depend on you. (Under-used)*

21. Go way above the call of duty. Your extra effort makes it obvious to TOS that you have their best interests at heart.

22. Go slightly above call of duty. Offer common courtesy and good manners, but don't go overboard.

23. Help TOS pay less. Try delayed payment terms, shipping discounts, slightly lower-quality products.

24. Ooze warmth. Be extraordinarily hospitable so that TOS feels comfortable.

Dirty Tricks

Act *before* the negotiating begins

1. *Trap TOS — make it impossible for them to go somewhere else at the last minute. Stall until just before their deadline, and then demand a lot more money. It's a con game. (Under-used)*

2. Get an invulnerable reputation. Brag and get others to brag about you. Say "I expect you to give in." If TOS can't find any weak spot, they will.

Act *after* the negotiating is over

3. *Sign the contract, and escalate immediately. Pause as you're signing and ask TOS for something extra — minor, not major. (Under-used)*

4. *Sign the contract, and re-negotiate immediately. Re-open bargaining right after you sign the contract. In many non-western nations, this is the norm. (Under-used)*

5. *Claim limited authority — You have to ask for permission first. Tentatively agree, then say "I need my boss's OK." (Over-used)*

6. Take revenge — ruin TOS's victory celebration. It's tempting to hurt the victor, but it's a waste of your energy.

Test TOS

7. Deliberately break minor rules early. Test TOS — see how far you can push their limits.

8. Deliberately make minor mistakes early. Once again, test TOS — see how far you can push their limits.

Deliberately act incompetent

9. Mix up dates on purpose. At the contract signing, say "I thought delivery was November 1. I can't meet your October 1 deadline."

10. Confuse net and gross profit on purpose. Play dumb and hope TOS doesn't notice your mistake in the contract.

11. Confuse simple and compound interest on purpose. Play dumb and hope TOS doesn't notice your mistake in the contract.

12. Subtly change contract specifications on purpose. Hope TOS doesn't notice.

13. Get something for nothing. Find a loophole in TOS's ad and exploit it.

14. Send TOS a phony bill (small amount) on purpose. The con artist hopes they don't notice and pay it. (Don't commit crimes)

15. Use the buyer's bait-and-switch tactic. Take advantage of the seller's mistake, and get something for almost nothing.

Use sneaky pricing

16. *Use the seller's bait-and-switch tactic. Make attractive promises. When TOS is ready to buy, say "I can't do that anymore — accept this instead." (Under-used)*

17. As a buyer, make a very high initial offer — the "High Ball." Offer to buy at a very high price. When the seller cuts off negotiations with the other buyers, say "I can't afford it." See if the buyer will lower the price.

18. As a buyer, make a very low initial offer with protections — the "Low Ball." Make the seller think you're an easy mark. They don't know your offered contract has hidden clauses to protect you.

Use and abuse the law

19. Bring a frivolous lawsuit to harass TOS. Make them spend money unnecessarily.

20. Bribe TOS. Offer them favors on the side. But is it legal? (Don't commit crimes.)

21. Blackmail TOS. Threaten to reveal embarrassing information about them. But is it legal? (Don't commit crimes.)

22. Watch for extortion, shakedowns. The con artist obtains valuable favors from TOS by force, threats, other criminal methods. (Don't commit crimes.)

Profit by espionage

23. Find out TOS's secrets legally. Use the internet, market research, detectives.

24. Find out TOS's secrets illegally. The con artist engages in a variety of tactics, from phishing to break-ins and stupidly ignores criminal penalties. (Don't commit crimes.)

Display an arrogant attitude

25. *Act untouchable — you're entitled. Get favors by claiming "Everybody gives me special privileges." (Under-used)*

26. Exhibit phony sanctimony. Act "holier-than-thou."

27. *Act smug — "I know you well." Make TOS think you already know a lot about them. Then ask questions to test their honesty. (Under-used)*

Wield words and spread rumors

28. Smear TOS. Guilt by alleged association. Make them vulnerable.

29. Isolate TOS. Use the grapevine to spread bad rumors about them. Make them vulnerable.

30. Isolate your competitors. Use the grapevine to spread bad rumors about them. Make them vulnerable.

Use psychological warfare

31. Humiliate and ridicule TOS. Try to demoralize them so they'll become vulnerable.

32. Glare and stare. Make TOS face the sun.

33. Give TOS a chair that's lower than yours.

34. Give TOS a chair that's unstable.

35. Create a steam bath — an intentionally hot conference room.

36. Create a freezer — an intentionally cold conference room.

37. Use your meeting room to intimidate — TOS's first impression is shock and awe at the décor.

38. *Use frightening ambience, manipulative music. Manipulate TOS this way. (Under-used)*

39. Run the marathon — all-night negotiating sessions.

40. Frequently change the meeting time to put TOS off-balance.

41. Employ the caterer from hell — serve lousy food and drinks.

42. Employ the caterer from hell again — The con artist intentionally gives TOS mild food poisoning. (Don't commit crimes.)

43. Have a dirty visitors' toilet — use the power of Y.U.C.K. (You Use Contaminated Krapper)

44. Leave bad smells in the meeting room. Intentionally bad odors — subtle ones.

45. Put up TOS in a Roach Motel (with terrible rooms).

46. Put TOS in the Twilight Zone. Puzzle TOS with very strange, weird actions.

47. Have many planned interruptions. Have many people enter the meeting unannounced.

48. Have unusually pleasant interruptions. Have attractive people enter the meeting, say nothing, leave after a while. Ignore them. Don't tell TOS why.

Resort to real warfare

49. Use the Stockholm Syndrome. Create a bond with TOS, and then exploit it.

50. Act extremely hostile and nasty. Be obviously antagonistic, even angry.

51. *Scare the hell out of TOS. Have a temper tantrum to make them fear you. (Over-used)*

52. Make TOS lose their temper. Irritate them to get them angry.

53. Resort to physical violence. The con artist uses brute force. (Don't commit crimes.)

Use dirty lies

54. Lie doubly. Back up your lies with misleading statistics.

55. *Lie obviously — don't just exaggerate. Big talk, no action. (Over-used)*

56. Lie about withdrawing from the deal. But hang around, hiding behind intermediaries.

Take advantage of gullibility and greed

57. Overbook appointments on purpose. Schedule several at same time.

58. Ask TOS, "Guess who was here? Guess who's coming by later?" Give them the names of their competitors you're seeing today.

59. See two competing buyers in two rooms at the same time.

60. Tell TOS that extreme shortages are coming soon. You can't supply all they want, so they'll buy more now and pay more.

61. Tell TOS that you'll soon drop this product. Tell them you won't be offering this anymore so they'll buy more now and pay more.

Watch for phishing scams (e-mail only)

62. The lottery winner scam. The con artist defrauds TOS by telling them they won the lottery. (Don't commit crimes.)

63. The Nigerian scam. The con artist defrauds TOS with a promise of big bucks. (Don't commit crimes.)

Watch for sympathy-seeking scams

64. Offers to sell magazine subscriptions at your front door scam. The con artist says "I'm a poor college student. Help me win a scholarship." (Don't commit crimes.)

65. The taxi money scam. The con artist says "My car won't start. It's an emergency. Please help me." (Don't commit crimes.)

66. The "please send me money at the airport" scam. The con artist sends an e-mail message that says "I lost my passport and money at the airport. Please help me." (Don't commit crimes.)

Watch for crash-and-bump scams

67. The car accident scam. The con artist has a minor car accident on purpose. TOS stops, and the con artist robs them. (Don't commit crimes.)

68. The dead camel on the road to Dubai scam. The con artist claims TOS hit and killed his camel, wants blood money. Similar to "You break it, you buy it" sign in stores. (Don't commit crimes.)

Watch for inspection scams

69. The bribe me, or I'll close you down for health violations scam. The con artist poses as a phony health inspector. (Don't commit crimes.)

70. The inspector with secret partner scam. The con artist finds building violations, suggests a contractor — the con artist's partner. (Don't commit crimes.)

Watch for tourist scams

71. The deposit for phony service scam. The con artist gets paid, promises to return to perform service, and never does. (Don't commit crimes.)

72. The avoid customs duty scam. On an overseas trip the con artist retailer fraudulently promises to mail merchandise so paying customer can avoid customs duty. (Don't commit crimes.)

73. The shakedown by phony cop scam. The con artist often uses this on tourists. (Don't commit crimes.)

Watch for sex scams

74. The "come meet my sister — she's a doctor" scam. The con artist arranges a meeting to rob TOS. (Don't commit crimes.)

75. The wild party invitation scam. The con artist asks TOS "There's a wild sex party tonight. Want to come?" They come and get robbed. (Don't commit crimes.)

Take advantage of the ultimate loser

76. *Take advantage of the ultimate loser's greed and gullibility. A deadly combination. (Over-used)*

Use other dirty tricks

77. *Deliberately embarrass TOS, but only slightly. Put them on the defensive. (Under-used)*

78. Deliberately gross-out TOS. Use mildly disgusting behavior.

79. Confuse TOS by using a famous name. The con artist adopts a name similar to a well-known person, company. (Don't commit crimes.)

80. Get TOS drunk or high. The con artist dulls TOS's senses and judgment by deliberately supplying alcohol or drugs. (Don't commit crimes.)

Finally, commit the dirtiest trick of all

81. Have a thick face, black heart. You pretend to negotiate in good faith, but you keep doing what you've been doing — you have no scruples.

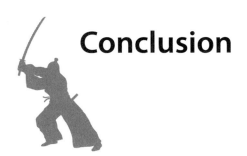

Conclusion

Well, do you feel like a warrior? Did your book give you the *killer instinct?* If so, which of the hundreds of weapons will you use when you battle your competitors for a larger market share and bigger profits? Here are what I think are the most important highlights of your book:

Chapter 1 — Basic Training

Business executives who master military strategy and tactics and use them get bigger market shares. Their sales and profits go way, way up. Chapter 1 helped you develop the killer instinct that turns innocent lambs into powerful business warriors who win big and win often! You learned that some people play this power game for money. Some for security or fame. Others for sex. But the master players seek power itself, because they know power can be used to obtain money, sex, security, or fame.

Chapter 2 — Strategy, Tactics, and Surprise

Strategy is deciding *what* to do. Tactics is deciding *how* to do it. You learned in Chapter 2 that the *winning-est* business warriors go after and conquer competitors who are easily conquered. They do this by distracting and deceiving their enemies, by confusing them, and by using tactics that work. Especially surprise tactics — play upon their fears, make them feel trapped. Make them make mistakes — and never interrupt them when they're making a mistake. In short, don't die for your country — make the other poor bastard die for his country!

Chapter 3 — Planning, War Games, and Winning Big

Following the 11 planning steps you learned in Chapter 3 will help you become the 800-pound gorilla in your industry. Some important highlights you should remember:

- How to become more decisive

- How to make good decisions without ulcers

- The "So what?" analysis — a new, improved version of SWAT analysis

- Eight overlooked gaps in the marketplace you can fill at a big profit

- Learn what your attitude toward risk is — are you a falcon, a sitting duck, a chicken, or a dodo bird?

- Going inside business simulations — some of the best war games on the market

Chapter 4 — Winning the Battle for Your Customer's Mind: The Three Ps of Marketing

No, not the well-known Four Ps. This chapter gave you unique insights into the Three *Powers* of marketing warfare — Positioning, Brand Personality, and Psychographics. Don't give up if your brand is weak — fortify it and you'll actually defeat attacks made by the market leader. Only losers attack this Big Dog head-on. Other important highlights:

- How to describe your brand as if it were a human being

- Share of mind — why it's so important to be first and what you can do if you're not first

- How to turn brand followers into big winners

Chapter 5 — Out-Thinking Your Competitors: The Creative Business Warrior

Most creative people share the 20 characteristics you learned in this chapter. How many of them do you have? If you have many, you can be the change agent for your company. Turn it into a creative powerhouse — you learned how to do it in this chapter. The best ways to transform you and your company include these techniques:

- Become more like a child.
- Brainstorm — a much, much better way than you've ever seen.
- Use forced relationships — learn from cartoonists.
- Put your judgment on hold using the PIN technique.
- Use a bug list.
- Think of 101 uses for ….
- Find creativity-stimulating exercises and do them.

Chapter 6 — The Four Battlegrounds of Business: All About Strategy

You learned here how to become the Big Dog in your market and how to stay on top in each business battleground you enter. The secret: Domination by cloaking yourself with the aura of vicious vulnerability. You got answers to these questions:

- Is your brand a star, problem child, cash cow, or dog? Simple math will tell you.
- How can you keep a star in orbit?
- How can you keep your cash cow pumping out that profitable milk?
- How can you strengthen and fortify your weak brands so that they can become cash cows?

Chapter 7 — Offensive and Defensive Weapons: All About Tactics

Reading this chapter prepared you for guerrilla warfare (chapter 8) and warfare the Big Dog's way (chapter 9). You found out what tactics work best in Battlegrounds 1, 2, 3, and 4. There are 70 of them — yes, 70. And you learned to master them here. They include:

- 8 maneuvering tactics
- 13 attacking tactics
- 11 pursuit tactics
- 11 defense tactics
- 18 retreat tactics
- And 9 rejuvenating tactics

And you also learned about:

- Enveloping attacks
- Frontal attacks
- Wing attacks
- Flanking attacks
- Guerrilla attacks
- The six stages of battle

Chapter 8 — Winning Business Warfare the Guerrilla Way: Getting Big by Thinking Small

In this chapter you found out that the ultimate Big Dog was founded by the ultimate guerrilla — Sam Walton! The story of how he used 22 of Mao Tse-Tung's guerrilla warfare tactics to turn Wal-Mart into the dominant retailer in the world surprised and intrigued you. You probably started thinking, "I'm going to do the same thing!" You will if you master the 43 tactics used in the three phases of guerrilla warfare:

- The early beginnings
- Direct, strong attacks
- The follow-the-leader phase

Chapter 9 — Winning Business Warfare the Big Dog's Way

There are six kinds of Big Dogs, and you learned in this chapter how to tell them apart. This is very valuable information. Why? Because the most successful business warriors know that each kind of Big Dog is most easily conquered by a different set of strategies and tactics. Some Big Dogs are so dominant, you'll never beat them. And some are on their last legs. You learned 52 out-of-the-box tactics you can use against any and all of these Big Dogs. If you master them and use them correctly, you'll increase your sales so much that you'll become a powerhouse in your market.

Chapter 10 — Hidden Gems You Didn't Learn in Marketing 101

What you read in this chapter was definitely not your father's four Ps. Here are some of the many valuable tools you learned in Chapter 10:

- Why new products fail and what you can do about it
- How to win a price war
- A high price or a low price — 16 rules-of-thumb
- Sales contests that really motivate your sales reps
- How to choose an ad agency that puts *your* interests first — 15 often-overlooked ways
- 24 precise techniques to choose the very best middlemen
- How to come up with the optimum blend of advertising and personal selling

Chapter 11 — 365 Winning Weapons

The chapter you just read gave you a concise list of the 365 most powerful tactical weapons picked by tens of thousands of executives who have attended my negotiating and marketing warfare seminars in 36 nations on six continents.

Here are the six groups of weapons:

- 31 preparation
- 121 assertive
- 92 defensive
- 16 submissive
- 24 cooperative
- 81 dirty tricks

Try them all out. You'll soon find the ones that work best for you when you wheel and deal on the job, when you buy and sell — and also in personal situations such as getting out of a traffic ticket, selling your car, and even sexual seduction.

A Final Word

I'd like to close your book with not just one, but two, traditional Irish friendship wishes:

> *May you have love that never ends,*
> *Lots of money, and lots of friends.*
> *Health be yours, whatever you do,*
> *And may God send many blessings to you!*
>
> *May you live as long as you want,*
> *And never want as long as you live.*

COMPANY AND BRAND INDEX

PEOPLE INDEX

SUBJECT INDEX

ABOUT DONALD WAYNE HENDON

The most unique information I have to share with my clients: Specific negotiation tactics — those most favored by executives from more than 60 nations. Advance knowledge of these Weapons prepares executives when they negotiate with people from these nations — and gives them the power to win more. You saw a small sample of these specific Weapons in Chapter 11, Figure 11.1.

Where did I get this information? I have given in-house and public seminars and done consulting in 36 nations on six continents where I have interacted with and coached over 60 nationalities. I'll be glad to send you a list of 100 of my major clients. Some of them are: McDonald's, Coca-Cola, Nissan, Johnson & Johnson, the Las Vegas Convention and Visitors Authority, Australian Association of National Advertisers, Association of Canadian Advertisers, Philippine Airlines, and, once upon a time, Jimmy Carter's peanut business. And here are some of my seminar offerings:

- Negotiating-persuasion-influence-power
- International negotiating
- Body language
- Marketing warfare, guerrilla marketing, marketing strategy, dumb marketing mistakes
- Management skills and tools
- Creativity and entrepreneurship
- Customer relations, service, salesmanship, sales management

I have written nine other books, published in 14 nations, 10 languages, along with several hundred other publications. Books: *Guerrilla Deal-Making, Donald Wayne Hendon's 365 Weapons, 365 Powerful Ways to Influence, Battling for Profits, How to Negotiate Worldwide, World-Class Negotiating, Cross-Cultural Business Negotiations, Classic Failures in Product Marketing,* and *American Advertising.* And several hundred articles in many different trade journals and academic journals.

UNIVERSITY TEACHING CAREER: I have had over 30 years full-time teaching at various universities in United States (13 states and Puerto Rico) and abroad (Australia, Canada, Mexico, Malaysia, Oman, Saudi Arabia, United Arab Emirates). The 13 states include: Texas, Arkansas, Louisiana, Alabama, Georgia, Tennessee, Florida, Nebraska, South Dakota, Wyoming, Utah, Nevada, Hawaii. I retired from full-time teaching in 2002 to devote myself to consulting, coaching, training, seminars, and writing books.

DEGREES: Ph.D. from the University of Texas at Austin (1971). MBA from the University of California at Berkeley (1964). BBA from The University of Texas at Austin (1962).

E-MAIL: Donald_Hendon@hotmail.com

POSTAL ADDRESS: P. O. Box 2624, Mesquite, Nevada 89024, USA. Mesquite is 80 miles from Las Vegas.

WEBSITES: www.GuerrillaDon.com and www.DonaldHendon.com. Click on GuerrillaDon.com to get more information about many subjects in your book and to play my free game, Negotiation Poker. Apps for this game and for Business Warrior Poker will soon be available.

GET YOUR FREE GIFT!

As Promised on the Front Cover…
Bonus — Get a Free Business Warrior Secrets Kit … A $97 Value

Highlights from the Best of Donald Wayne Hendon's Seminars

Learn practical and powerful ideas that are guaranteed to *transform* your career

You'll get highlights from these 10 seminars:

- The prism of power — how to get others to do what you want them to do
- Winning entrepreneurship — how to start your own business and make lots of money
- How to improve your efficiency at work and at home
- How to deal with difficult people — good conflict and bad conflict
- How to set and achieve your lifetime goals
- How to get ahead in your career — quickly
- Time mastery — finally, the best way to manage your time
- Battling for profits — how to win in marketing warfare
- How to be more creative
- How to make decisions and solve problems without ulcers

To get these 10 highlights free right now, go to:
www.GuerrillaDon.com/FreeHighlights